OCS Study
MMS 2001-054

Coastal Marine Institute

Dispersion in Broad, Shallow Estuaries:
A Model Study

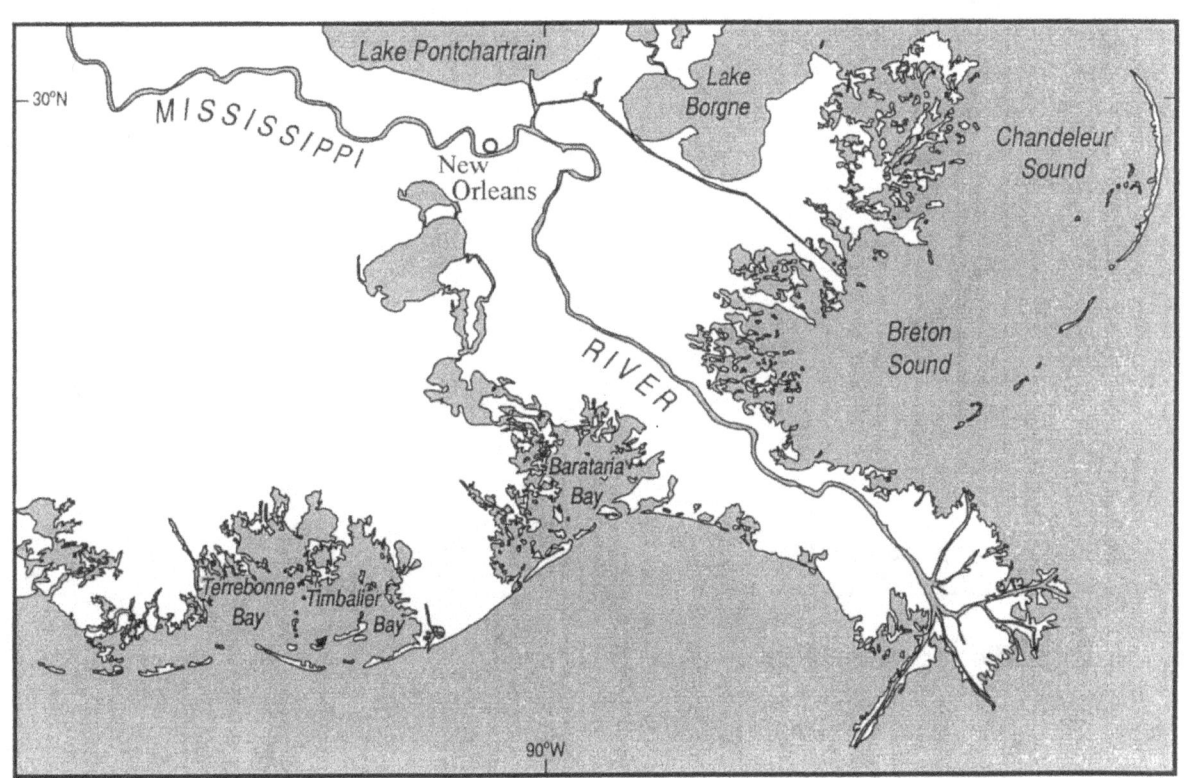

U.S. Department of the Interior
Minerals Management Service
Gulf of Mexico OCS Region

Cooperative Agreement
Coastal Marine Institute
Louisiana State University

OCS Study
MMS 2001-054

Coastal Marine Institute

Dispersion in Broad, Shallow Estuaries: A Model Study

Authors

Masamichi Inoue
William J. Wiseman, Jr.
Dongho Park
Dubravko Justic
Gregg Stone

July 2001

Prepared under MMS Contract
14-35-0001-30660-19953
by
Coastal Studies Institute
Louisiana State University
Baton Rouge, Louisiana 70801

Published by

U.S. Department of the Interior
Minerals Management Service
Gulf of Mexico OCS Region

Cooperative Agreement
Coastal Marine Institute
Louisiana State University

DISCLAIMER

This report was prepared under contract between the Minerals Management Service (MMS) and Louisiana State University. This report has been technically reviewed by the MMS and approved for publication. Approval does not signify that the contents necessarily reflect the view and policies of the Service nor does mention of trade names or commercial products constitute endorsement or recommendation for use. It is, however, exempt from review and compliance with MMS editorial standards.

REPORT AVAILABILITY

Extra copies of the report may be obtained from the Public Information Office (MS 5034) at the following address:

U.S. Department of the Interior
Minerals Management Service
Public Information Office (MS 5034)
Gulf of Mexico OCS Region
1201 Elmwood Park Boulevard
New Orleans, Louisiana 70123-2394

Telephone Number: (504) 736-2519
1-800-200-GULF

CITATION

Suggested citation:

Inoue, M., W. J. Wiseman, Jr., D. Park, D. Justic, and G. Stone. 2001. Dispersion in Broad, Shallow Estuaries: A Model Study. OCS Study MMS 2001-054. U.S. Dept. of the Interior, Minerals Management Service, Gulf of Mexico OCS Region, New Orleans, La. 54 pp.

ABSTRACT

Summary of our continuing effort under Coastal Marine Environmental Modeling: Part II is presented here. Coastal Marine Environmental Modeling targets the development of numerical models of estuarine shelf interactions with the ultimate objectives of formulating an coupled hydrodynamic-ecological model that includes biological and sedimentological components. Under Part II, there are three components covered in this report; an application of a previously developed two-dimensional depth-integrated hydrodynamic model, an enhancement of the depth-integrated hydrodynamic model, and a field program to measure currents and suspended sediments. Specifically, this report covers the following subjects; 1) a comparative model study of Barataria Basin, Louisiana, to delineate the role of wind forcing on flushing and dispersion characteristics, 2) an enhancement of the two-dimensional depth-integrated hydrodynamic model to include baroclinic pressure gradient; 3) the preliminary results of the first field deployment in Terrebonne Bay to measure currents and suspended sediments. The purpose of the field deployment is to document the role of waves and currents on sediment resuspension and eventually allow development and calibration of a suspended sediment module to be coupled to the hydrodynamic model. Significant role of wind forcing on flushing and dispersion characteristics of Barataria Basin is clearly demonstrated for the typical summer condition investigated. Flushing times for various subbasins were shorter by 20-40% under wind forced conditions compared to without wind. The impact of wind forcing becomes more prominent where the tidal energy is higher and the local geomorphology is complex. An accurate advection scheme is employed for advective transport of temperature and salinity. The hydrodynamic model that includes baroclinic pressure gradient has been successfully applied to Breton Sound. From the isolated measurements conducted so far, it is clear that wave-induced sediment resuspension is an important and poorly understood process within the shallow coastal bays of Louisiana. Of particular interest will be the importance of oceanic swell during pre-frontal winter conditions in resuspending bay bottom sediments.

TABLE OF CONTENTS

LIST OF FIGURES

LIST OF TABLES

ACKNOWLEDGMENTS

We would like to thank the Coastal Marine Institute at LSU that is funded by the Minerals Management Service for providing the necessary support for this project. The field component of this project would not have been possible without the excellent efforts by the Coastal Studies Institute Field Support Group. Assistance from many people including Erick M. Swenson in providing observed tide data for Barataria Basin, by S. A. Hsu and Brian Blanchard in suggesting a formula to convert from wind speed to wind stress is greatly appreciated. We thank Enrique Reyes for providing flow rate data at Caernarvon diversion. We thank Aleric Haaq for maintaining the network and the computing facilities at CSI.

CHAPTER 1

EFFECT OF WIND FORCING
ON FLUSHING AND DISPERSION CHARACTERISTICS OF BARATARIA BASIN

1.1 Introduction

Previously, a two-dimensional depth-integrated hydrodynamic model was developed and applied to estuaries in Louisiana (Inoue et al., 1998). Specifically, dispersion and flushing characteristics of Terrebonne/Timbalier Basin and Barataria Basin were examined using the hydrodynamic model forced by observed winds and tides. Since the previous study (Inoue et al., 1998) addressed only the combined impact of the wind and tidal forcings on the flushing and dispersion characteristics of those estuaries, relative impact of wind forcing versus that of tides needs to be examined. That is the topic to be addressed in this chapter.

The same two-dimensional, depth-integrated hydrodynamic model (Inoue et al., 1998) applied to the Barataria Basin, located just west of the Mississippi Delta (Figure 1-1), is used here. Barataria Basin is a relatively shallow estuary ranging from 1 to 3 m in depth, is very complicated geometrically and is connected to small lakes or ponds by several channels of varying width. It is further divided into a number of bays by low marshy islands of varying size. Into these areas the tide from the Gulf of Mexico enters through five main passes: Caminada Pass, Barataria Pass, Pass Abel, Quatre Bayou Pass, and Grand Bayou Pass. Water flow through the basin is highly variable. The dominant water exchange route between the upper and lower basin is through Little Lake, Bayou Perot and Lake Salvador. Secondary exchange is through Mud Lake and Barataria Bay Waterway. This is a micro-tidal environment with a typical tidal range of 0.3~0.6 m. Winds are typically from southeat during summer, and during winter, winds are characterized by the passage of cold fronts at intervals of a few days. Detailed background information on the environmental characteristics of Barataria Basin can be found in our previous report (Inoue et al., 1998).

The model domain used is shown in Figure 1-1. A spatially uniform model grid size (between like variables) of 463 m was adopted. The time step used is 10 s, and the horizontal eddy viscosity chosen is 10 m^2 s^{-1}. The model is forced by wind measured at Grand Isle C-MAN Station (shown in Figure 1-2) and sea-level heights along the open boundary located along the southern boundary of the model domain. Historical water level from 1988 collected by the US Army Corps of Engineers (USACOE), were used to estimate the sea-level height at the open boundary. The model was spun up from rest for the period 07/07/88-07/27/88, a typical summer condition (Figure 1-3). The first 10 days of simulation (07/07/88-07/17/88) were considered to be a spin-up period, and the following 10 days of simulation (07/17/88-07/27/88) output were analyzed. After a careful model calibration and testing, a Manning's coefficient of 0.04 was chosen for bottom friction.

2

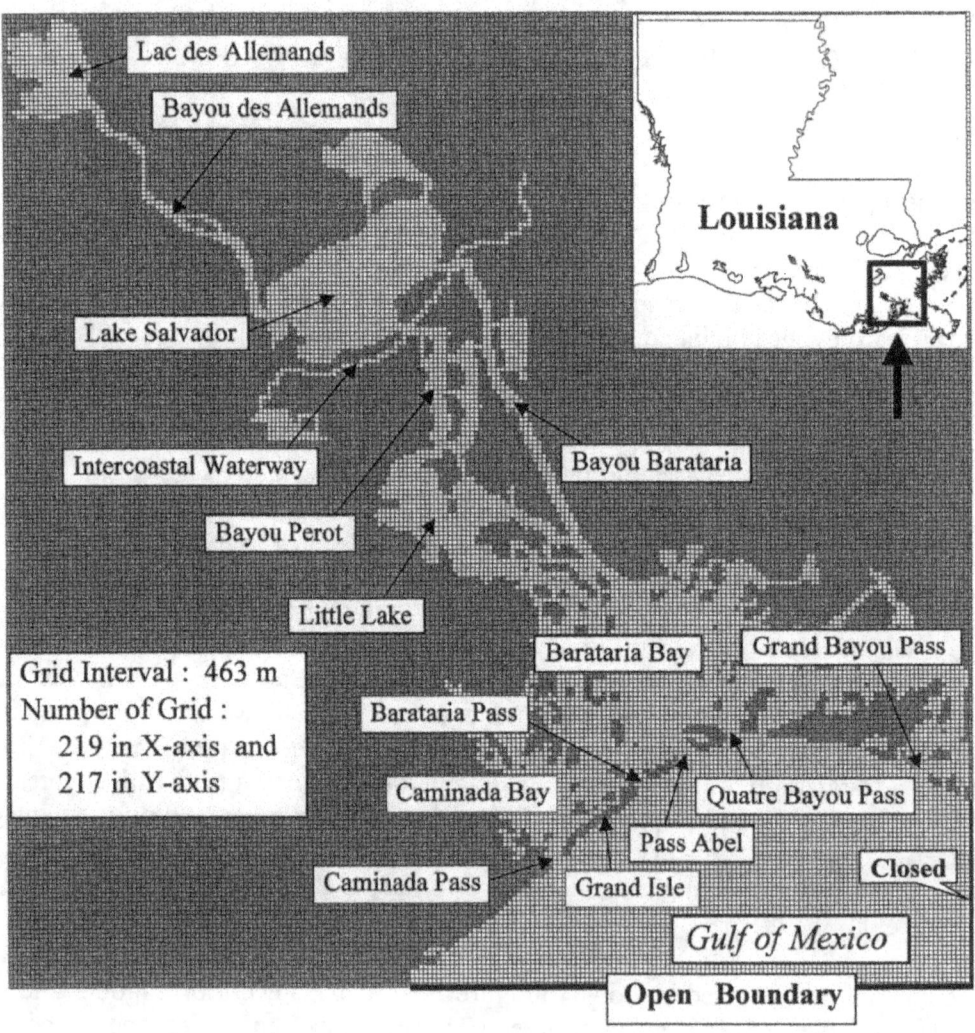

Figure 1-1. Location map of Barataria Basin and model domain used. Open boundary conditions are used along the southern boundary (taken from Inoue et al. (1998)).

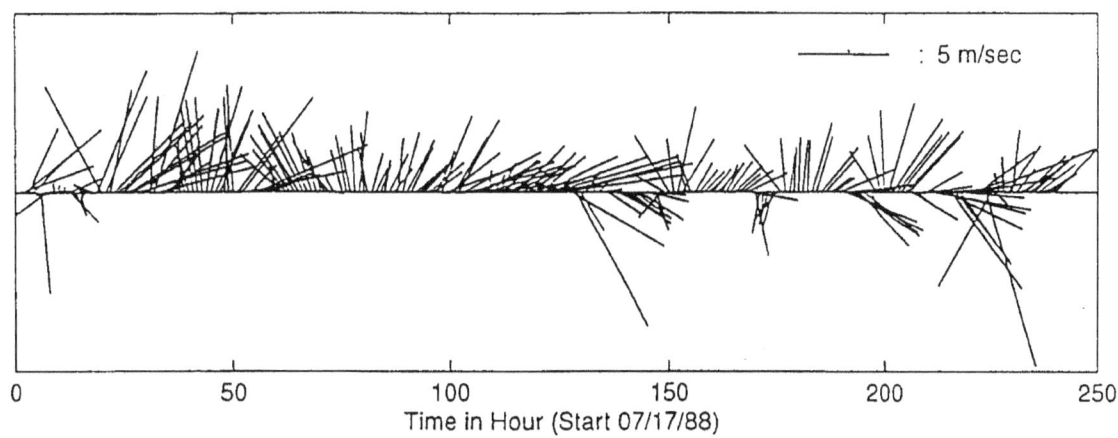

Figure 1-2. Wind vectors observed at Grand Isle for the period 07/17/88-07/27/88 (taken from Inoue et al. (1998)). North is upward.

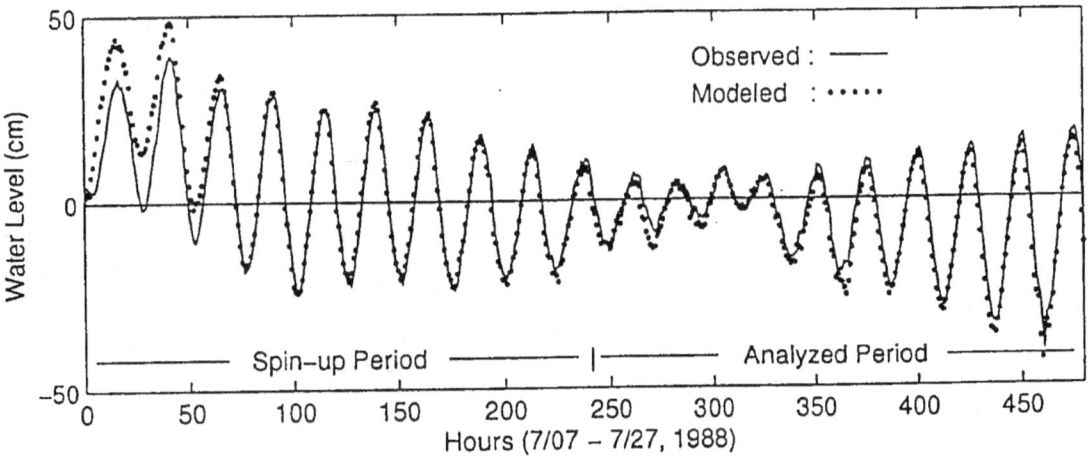

Figure 1-3. Comparison of the computed (dotted) and observed (solid) water level at the mouth of Barataria Bay (taken from Inoue et al. (1998)).

4

1.2 Model Simulation With and Without Wind Forcing

In order to examine flushing and dispersion characteristics, a Lagrangian technique (e. g., Awaji et al., 1980; Awaji, 1982; Ridderinkhof, 1990; Signell and Butman, 1992; Kapolnai et al., 1996) is employed. Various locations within the model domain were seeded with floating tracer particles and their subsequent trajectories were tracked. For each cluster of tracer particles, the variances of the particle positions $\sigma^2{}_x$ and $\sigma^2{}_Y$ along the major and minor axes of the cluster ellipse can be computed. The dispersive characteristics of a water mass can be described by the time evolution of these variances. The horizontal diffusivities K_x and K_Y along the major and minor axes are given by (Okubo, 1971),

$$K_X = \frac{1}{2}\frac{d}{dt}\sigma^2 x, \quad K_Y = \frac{1}{2}\frac{d}{dt}\sigma^2{}_Y$$

The mean horizontal diffusivity K_{XY} is defined as

$$K_{XY} = \frac{1}{2}\frac{d}{dt}\sigma_X\sigma_Y.$$

As was shown previously (e. g., Ridderinkhof, 1990), dispersive characteristics of a water mass are strongly dependent on time and space due to the significant spatial and temporal variations in the velocity field of the basin of interest.

To illustrate the dispersion characteristics for Barataria Basin, 49 tracer particles were initially released near the center of different areas of the model in a 7 by 7 array and followed under conditions with and without wind forcing. The initial position of each particle corresponds to a grid point. Figures 1-4a through 1-4d show particle locations at time of release (left) and after 10 days without wind forcing (middle) and with wind forcing (right) of these 49 tracer particles in Lake Salvador, Little Lake, Barataria Bay, and Caminada Bay, respectively.

At upstream sites, Lake Salvador and Little Lake, the shape of the cluster in both forcing situations showed a relatively small change with little distortion and maintenance of the main axes along the tidal current direction through the 10 days (Figs. 1-4a and 1-4b). The size of clusters in these two areas remained compact due not only to weak shear velocity and turbulence but also to the weak effect of tidal forcing. Table 1-1 compares the final cluster size between model runs and with the initial cluster. The presence of wind forcing doubled the cluster size in both areas. Further downstream, in Barataria Bay and Caminada Bay, the shape and size of the final cluster in the two forcing cases show totally different results (Figs. 1-4c and 1-4d). In Barataria Bay, the size of the cluster after 10 days without wind forcing is nearly three times bigger than the initial release due to particle separation caused by coastline irregularities trapping some particles (hereafter referred to as "coastal trapping" (Inoue et al., 1998)). With wind forcing the final cluster size was twenty-six times larger than without wind forcing, apparently due to coastal trapping and particle separation caused by islands (hereafter referred to as "island trapping"). In general, in the broad lower part of the Barataria Basin system, the combined impact of wind forcing and coastal trapping results in significant increases in particle

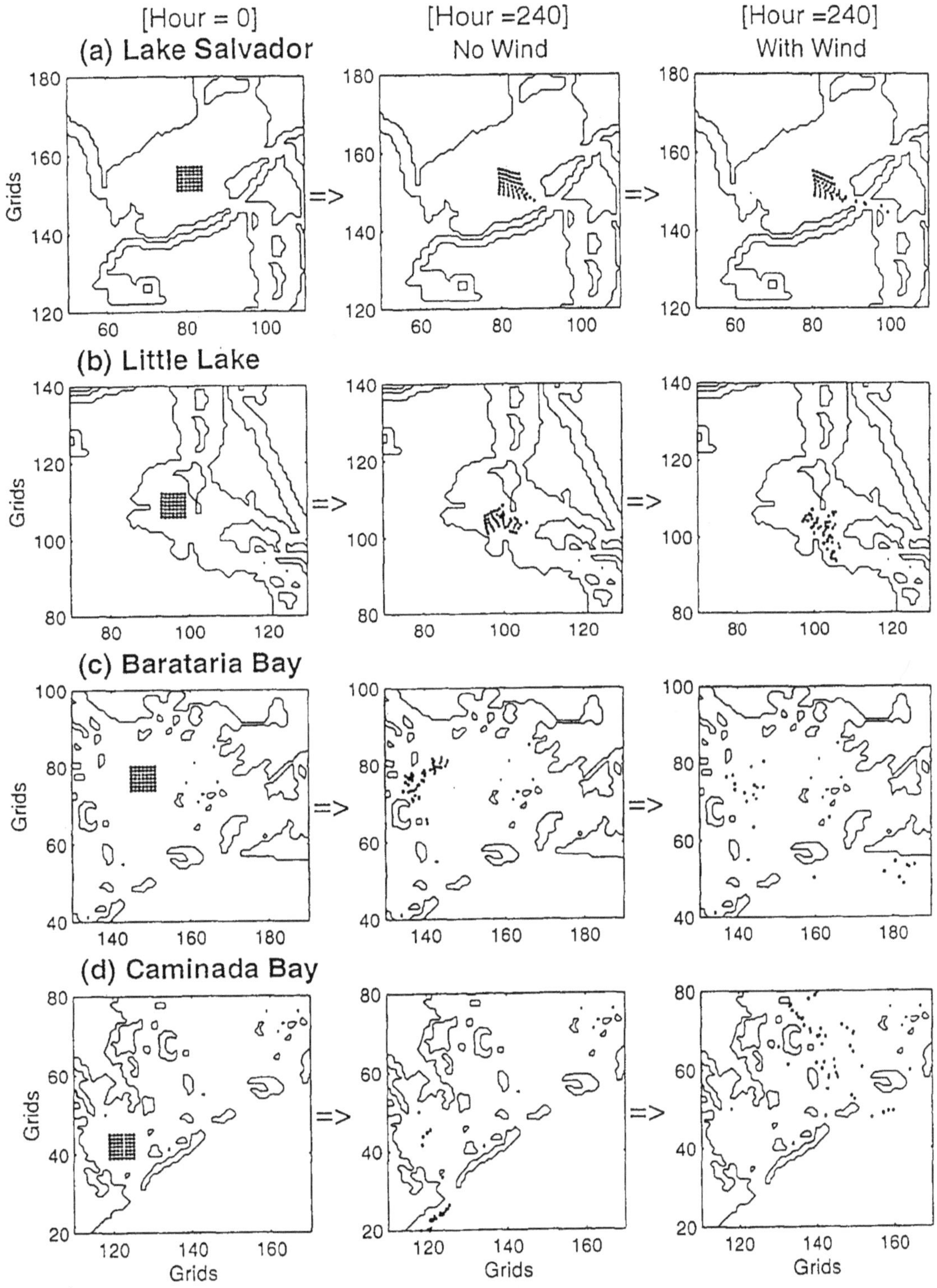

[Hour = 0]
(a) Lake Salvador

[Hour =240]
No Wind

[Hour =240]
With Wind

(b) Little Lake

(c) Barataria Bay

(d) Caminada Bay

Grids

Figure 1-4. A subset of tracer particles of 7 by 7 array at four areas of initial release (07/17/88: left), after 10 days without wind (middle), and with wind (right). Grid size is 463 m.

Table 1-1.
The ratio of cluster size between initial and after 10 days of simulation
without wind and with wind.

	Ratio of Cluster Size		
	No Wind/Initial	With Wind/Initial	With Wind/No Wind
Lake Salvador	1.27	2.64	2.08
Little Lake	1.23	2.45	1.91
Barataria Bay	2.91	75.71	26.02
Caminada Bay	3.52	20.61	5.86

dispersion. Byrne et al. (1976) and Banas (1978) found that when wind stress is included, the water renewal times in Barataria Basin decreased eight-fold. In Caminada Bay without wind forcing, the shape of the final cluster is significantly different from other cases due to coastal trapping and island separation. When the southwesterly wind was blowing, all of the particles moved to the neighboring Barataria Bay and the cluster size increased significantly due to coastal trapping and island separation. An apparent variance, $\sigma_X \sigma_Y$, as a function of time without wind and with wind forcing was computed. Figures 1-5a and 1-5b indicate the time evolution of $\sigma_X \sigma_Y$ for those tracer particles shown in Figs. 1-4a through 1-4d. Even with the wind forcing included, the average rates of dispersion in the four areas for the 10 days of simulation, as measured by the horizontal diffusivities, were 0.66 m^2 s^{-1} for Lake Salvador, 0.61 m^2 s^{-1} for Little Lake, 18.78 m^2 s^{-1} for Barataria Bay, and 5.92 m^2 s^{-1} for Caminada Bay.

In comparison to the diffusion coefficient diagram compiled by Okubo (1974) based on dye patch diffusion and float dispersion, the values obtained here are comparable (Figure. 1-6). Always, the horizontal diffusivity estimates with wind forcing were greater than those with no wind forcing. The results of calculations without wind forcing fall slightly below Okubo's range. In Barataria Bay and Caminada Bay, the results with wind forcing fall within Okubo's range. In the other two areas, Lake Salvador and Little Lake, the results are slightly lower than Okubo's range. As noted previously (Inoue et al., 1998), the larger values appear to be due to coastal topographic trapping and island separation. Enhancement of horizontal dispersion by coastal topographic trapping is due to the presence of critical points in the flow field near a coastal boundary where a small difference in the particle position leads to a large difference in the subsequent trajectory. An analytical model to explain the enhancement of dispersion in estuaries due to the entrapment by shoreline irregularities was first proposed by Okubo (1973). Signell et al. (1990) investigated the influence of a headland on horizontal dispersion using a depth-integrated numerical model. They found that the intense shear zone associated with the flow separation at the tip of the headland is responsible for explosive dispersion. Similar critical points in the flow field can be found near an island. The interaction of an oscillating tidal flow around an island can lead to the enhancement of particle dispersion, i.e., "island trapping." Recently, Sanderson et al. (1995) demonstrated that the particle dispersion away from island obstacles is an order of magnitude less than that due to an oscillating flow around islands. An example of the "island trapping" effect, can be found in Figs. 1-4c and 1-4d. These observations suggest that coastal trapping that includes not only trapping by shoreline irregularities, such as headlands and inlets, but also trapping by islands can significantly enhance particle dispersion. Similarly, Wolanski and Ridd (1986) have shown that tidal trapping in the swamps of mangrove estuaries can enhance longitudinal dispersion of nutrients and other materials by temporarily storing water in the swamps during the late flood and releasing it to a different part of the main flow during the ebb.

1.3 Flushing Characteristics

Flushing characteristics are analyzed by computing residence time that defines the average time water particles remain in an area. This is an important measure for many practical

8

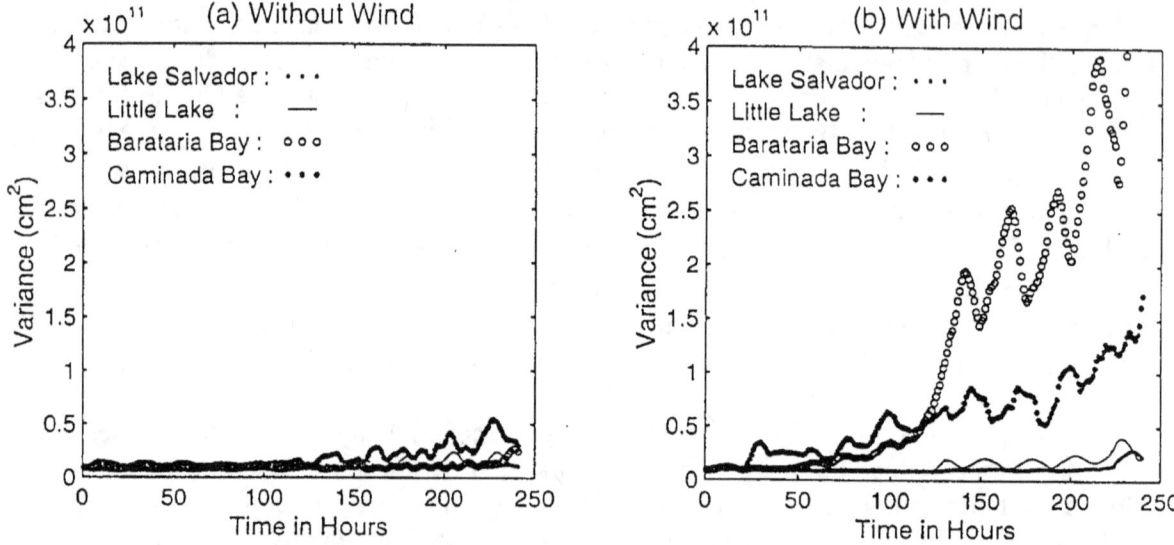

Figure 1-5. Variance of particle cluster size, $\sigma_X\sigma_Y$, versus time for the 49 particle cluster at four areas shown in Figure 1-4 without wind (left) and with wind (right).

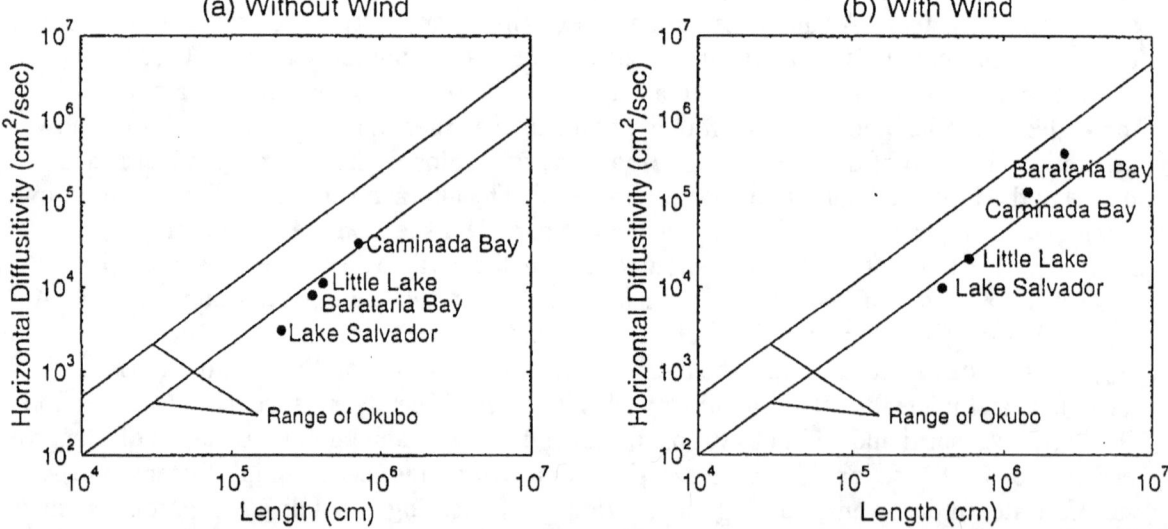

Figure 1-6. Horizontal diffusivities (cm^2s^{-1}) of 49 particles released at various locations versus scale of diffusion, $l = 3\sqrt{2\sigma_X\sigma_Y}$ without wind (left) and with wind (right). Range of Okubo's data (1974) is bounded by two solid lines, $0.01\left(\dfrac{l^2}{9}\right)^{\frac{2}{3}}$ and $0.002\left(\dfrac{l^2}{9}\right)^{\frac{2}{3}}$ (Fisher et al., 1979).

problems such as the dispersion of suspended sediments, pollutants, and floating biological particles. In order to shed light on the spatial variability of this parameter, labeled tracer particles were released in the model to represent water particles, and their trajectories were continuously tracked.

For this experiment, the same simulation period used in the previous section was considered. After a model spin-up of ten simulation days, 5,884 particles were initially released with one particle at every grid point throughout the domain. Then, the trajectories of the particles were tracked for the next 10 simulation days. The Lagrangian movements of the labeled particles clearly indicate the principal flow paths associated with subtidal circulation. For the simulation period examined, subtidal circulation includes a consistent inflow through Caminada Pass. A consistent outflow takes place through the other main passes. It should be noted that the winds, though variable, were dominantly from the southwest. Wind appears to dictate the flushing characteristics. Specifically, a considerable number of particles from Caminada Bay moved to the neighboring Barataria Bay in a couple of days. It appears that the combined impact of winds and tides enhanced the particles' movement northeastward. After 10 days, roughly 60 % of the particles moved to Barataria Bay from Caminada Bay. Generally, the further north one goes up the system the slower movements become.

Often it is meaningful to evaluate flushing time for various regions within the whole system. Therefore, the system was subdivided into eight subbasins. Figures 1-7a through 1-7h show particles as initially released (left), after 10 days without wind forcing (middle) and with wind forcing (right), in the eight subbasins. Ridderinkhof (1990) defined the flushing time as the time required to flush out a fraction $1 - e^{-1}$ (=0.632, i. e., 63.2%) of the particles initially deployed inside the bay. The flushing time for the eight subbasins ranges from 48.4 to 14.4 days without wind forcing and from 9.0 to 38.1 days with wind forcing (Table 1-2). When wind influence was added, the flushing time decreased by 20 to 40 %. Generally, it takes much longer to flush lakes in the upstream region, such as Lac des Allemands (38.1 days) and Lake Salvador (38.5 days) than canals and waterways, such as Bayou des Allemands (22.4 days), Bayou Perot and Bayou Rigolettes (12.4 days), Bayou Barataria (20.4 days), and Little Lake and Turtle Bay (15.0 days).

Higher tidal ranges will be associated with shorter flushing times and smaller tidal ranges with longer flushing times (Wiseman and Swenson, 1989). Wind forcing will also enhance flushing. For instance, Banas (1978) estimated that it takes 11.6 days with wind and 135 days without wind to flush Barataria Bay. Byrne et al. (1976) found that 80 diurnal cycles with wind forcing and 640 diurnal cycles without wind forcing were required for a 99 % volume change in the Barataria Basin Management Unit. Wiseman and Swenson (1989) found a 90 % renewal time, less than about 53 days (1.75 months), for Barataria Basin using a tidal prism model. Our estimate showed a 14 % renewal after 10 days for Barataria Basin. This implies a 90 % renewal time of about 65 days assuming a linear extrapolation. These values are surprisingly comparable considering that some estimates included wind forcing while others do not and that the winds considered differ amongst authors.

10

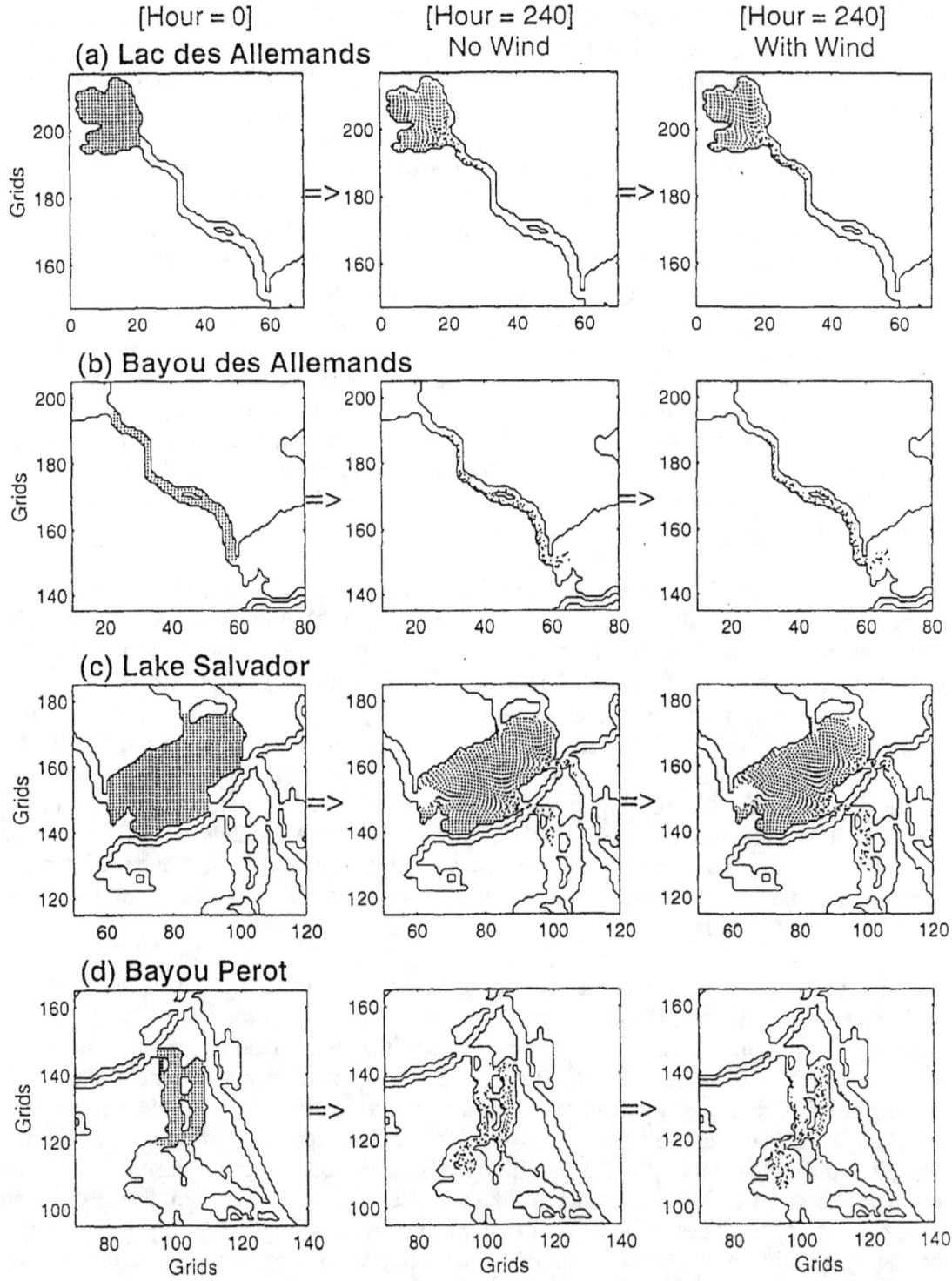

Figure 1-7. Tracer particles at time of release (07/17/88: left), after 10 days without wind (middle), and with wind (right) at eight subbasins of Barataria Basin. Grid size is 463 m.

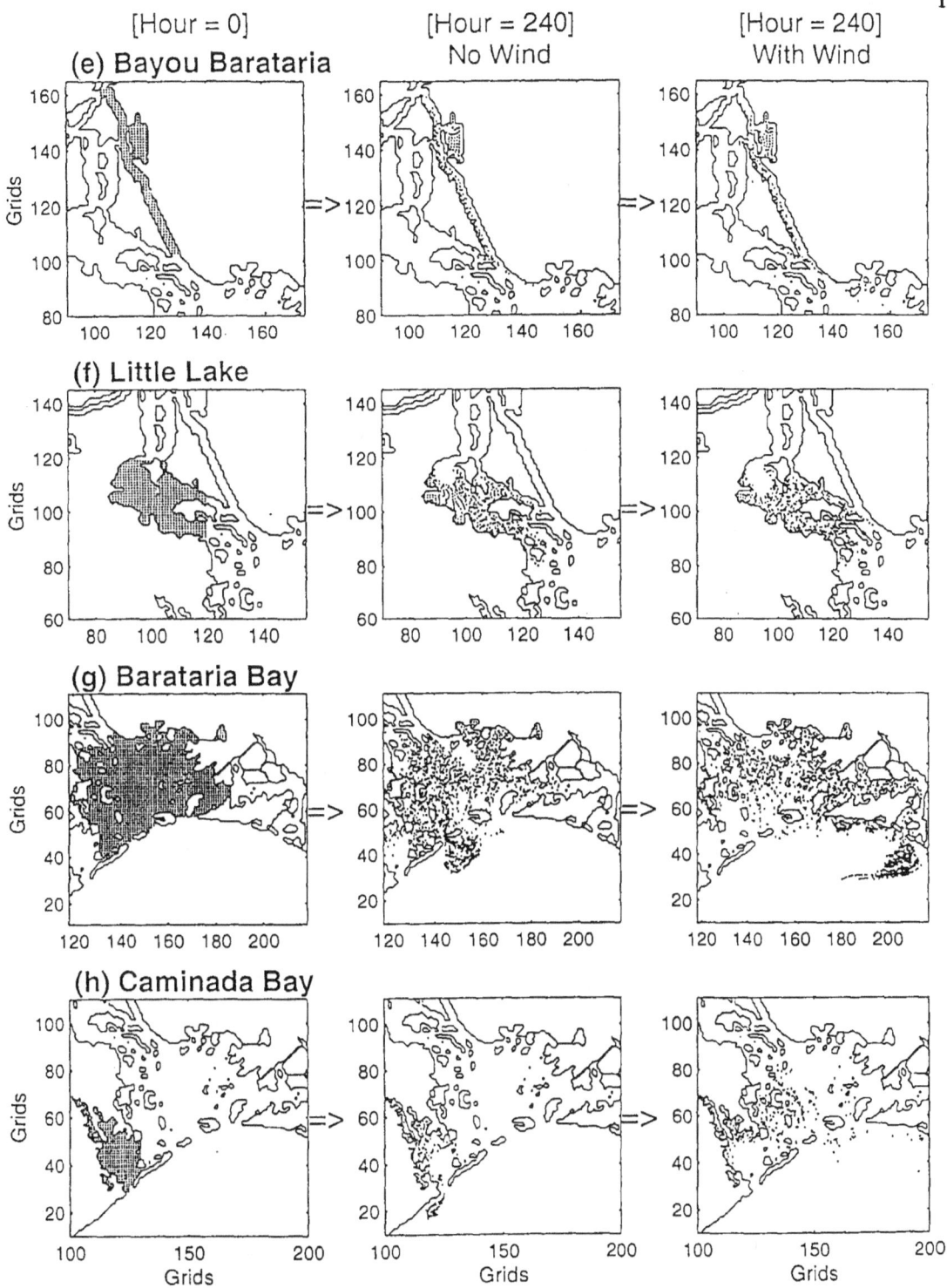

Figure 1-7. Tracer particles at time of release (07/17/88: left), after 10 days without wind (middle), and with wind (right) at eight subbasins of Barataria Basin. Grid size is 463m

Table 1-2.
Estimated flushing time for eight subbasins.

	No Wind Flushing Time (Days)	With Wind Flushing Time (Days)
Lac des Allemands	48.4	38.1
Bayou des Allemands	29.5	22.4
Lake Salvador	48.1	34.3
Bayou Perot	16.1	12.8
Bayou Barataria	27.0	20.4
Little Lake	19.1	15.0
Barataria Bay	17.7	12.3
Caminada Bay	14.4	9.0

1.4 Summary and Conclusions

Using the previously applied and tested depth-integrated hydrodynamic model, the objective here is to delineate the role of wind forcing in flushing and dispersion characteristics of Barataria Basin under a typical summer condition. The model was forced by the observed tide with and without wind forcing. A Lagrangian technique, whereby the model was seeded with a number of tracer particles, and the trajectories of those particles were tracked, was utilized to estimate rate of particle dispersion and flushing time. Computed estimates of particle patch variance, $\sigma_X \sigma_Y$, as a function of time, t, show that the estimated diffusivities generally fall within the range of diffusivities estimated by Okubo (1974) for both conditions. Diffusivity values slightly below Okubo's range correspond to conditions without wind forcing. Wind forcing enhances diffusivity values. In particular, wind forcing in combination with coastal and island trapping gives rise to the highest diffusivity values. With wind forcing included, estimated flushing time varies from approximately 10 days in the downstream subbasins to more then 30 days in the upstream subbasins (Inoue et al., 1998). In contrast, the flushing times for various subbasins were shorter by 20-40 % under wind forced conditions compared to without wind forcing. Overall, wind forcing enhances flushing and dispersion characteristics significantly if it is combined with higher tidal energy and more complex geomorphology.

CHAPTER 2

AN ENHANCEMENT OF A DEPTH-INTEGRATED TWO-DIMENSIONAL
HYDRODYNAMIC MODEL TO INCLUDE BAROCLINIC PRESSURE GRADIENT

2.1 Background

During the initial phase of this modeling effort, a two-dimensional depth-integrated
hydrodynamic model was formulated and applied to Terrebonne/Timbalier Basin as well as
Barataria Basin (Inoue et al., 1998). In this chapter, an enhancement of the hydrodynamic
model to include baroclinic pressure gradient, is described. The model used here is based on
the model initially developed for other neighboring estuaries including Terrebonne-
Timbalier Basin (Inoue and Wiseman, 2000), Fourleague Bay (Wiseman and Inoue, 1994),
and Barataria Basin (Park, 1998).

One of the novel features of the present enhancement of the model is the incorporation of
a very accurate advection scheme. Traditionally, a simple centered-difference scheme has
been used for advective transport in hydrodynamic models. This scheme induces so-called
numerical dispersion, which causes nonphysical spatial oscillation in the tracer field
(Hasumi and Suginohara, 1999). These oscillations could be damped out by using a large
diffusion coefficient. However, as the model grid size is reduced to resolve finer and finer
spatial scales, the use of large diffusion coefficients is no longer justified. Some
hydrodynamic models adopt the upstream or the weighted upstream scheme for advective
transport (e. g., Maier-Reimer et al., 1993). These schemes do not induce nonphysical
oscillation. Instead, their accuracy is lower than that of the centered differencing scheme,
and the effect of the error is to enhance diffusion. There have been several schemes
developed that have little numerical dispersion and a higher order of accuracy compared
with the centered differencing scheme. One of the most accurate schemes to date is the flux-
corrected transport (FCT) scheme of Boris and Book (1973). However, the FCT scheme
could double computational costs compared to the centered-differencing or the upstream
scheme (Gerdes et al., 1991). There are some less expensive alternative schemes: the
Uniformly Third-Order Polynominal Interpolation Algorithm (UTOPIA; Leonard et al.,
1993), the Quadratic Upstream Interpolation for Convective Kinematics (QUICK; Leonard
1979; Farrow and Stevens 1995) and the Multidimensional Positive Definite Advection
Transport Algorithm (MPDATA; Smolarkiewicz 1984). They have the same or higher
order of accuracy as compared with the centered differencing scheme, and exhibit little
numerical dispersion. In this study, an advection scheme due to Hsu and Arakawa (1990) is
adopted (herafter referred to as Hsu-Arakawa scheme), which was based on the Takacs
scheme (1985). This scheme is an upstream scheme. However, this scheme completely
eliminates unrealistic negative values, and its computational cost is reasonable.

2.2 Numerical Model Formulation

The model equations for conservation of mass and momentum including baroclinic pressure gradient written in Cartesian coordinates in terms of depth-integrated transport (e. g., Leendertse, 1967; Elliott and Reid, 1976) are;

$$\frac{\partial U}{\partial t} + \frac{\partial}{\partial x}\frac{U^2}{H} + \frac{\partial}{\partial y}\frac{UV}{H} - fV = -gH\frac{\partial \zeta}{\partial x} - \frac{1}{2}gH^2\frac{\partial \rho}{\partial x} - g\frac{\frac{U}{H}\left\{\left(\frac{U}{H}\right)^2 + \left(\frac{V}{H}\right)^2\right\}^{\frac{1}{2}}}{C^2} + \frac{\tau_x}{\rho} + A\nabla^2 U$$

$$\frac{\partial V}{\partial t} + \frac{\partial}{\partial x}\frac{UV}{H} + \frac{\partial}{\partial y}\frac{V^2}{H} + fU = -gH\frac{\partial \zeta}{\partial y} - \frac{1}{2}gH^2\frac{\partial \rho}{\partial y} - g\frac{\frac{V}{H}\left\{\left(\frac{U}{H}\right)^2 + \left(\frac{V}{H}\right)^2\right\}^{\frac{1}{2}}}{C^2} + \frac{\tau_y}{\rho} + A\nabla^2 V$$

$$\frac{\partial \zeta}{\partial t} + \frac{\partial U}{\partial x} + \frac{\partial V}{\partial y} = 0$$

$$\frac{\partial HS}{\partial t} + \frac{\partial HS}{\partial x} + \frac{\partial HS}{\partial y} = D_s\left(\frac{\partial H\frac{\partial S}{\partial x}}{\partial x} + \frac{\partial H\frac{\partial S}{\partial y}}{\partial y}\right)$$

$$\frac{\partial HT}{\partial t} + \frac{\partial HT}{\partial x} + \frac{\partial HT}{\partial y} = D_T\left(\frac{\partial H\frac{\partial T}{\partial x}}{\partial x} + \frac{\partial H\frac{\partial T}{\partial y}}{\partial y}\right)$$

where $\quad U = \int_{-h}^{\zeta} u\,dz$

$$V = \int_{-h}^{\zeta} v\,dz$$

$$H = h + \zeta$$

$$S = \frac{1}{H}\int_{-h}^{\zeta} s(z)\,dz$$

$$T = \frac{1}{H}\int_{-h}^{\zeta} t(z)\,dz$$

where t denotes time, x, y, and z are Cartesian coordinates, u and v denote velocity components in the direction of x and y, respectively, ζ is elevation of the free surface above mean sea level, h is the undisturbed depth of the water, f is the Coriolis parameter (assumed to be a constant), g is the acceleration due to gravity, τ_x and τ_y are the x and y components of wind stress, respectively, ρ is the density of water, s(z) and t(z) are depth-dependent salinity and temperature, respectively, A is the horizontal eddy viscosity, S is depth-averaged salinity, T is depth-averaged temperature, D_S and D_T are the horizontal eddy diffusivities for S and T, respectively, and C is the Chezy coefficient which is depth dependent. The bottom roughness is represented through Manning's n coefficient, such that the Chezy coefficient is evaluated as

$$C = \frac{1}{n} H^{\frac{1}{6}}$$

At land boundaries, no normal flow and no-slip boundary conditions are used. Wind forcing is assumed to be spatially uniform over the entire model domain.

The following equation of state relating temperature and salinity to density of sea water at one standard atmospheric pressure is adopted (UNESCO, 1981). The shallowness of the basin under investigation allows the exclusion of the effect of pressure on density.

$$\rho = 999.842594 + 6.793952 \times 10^{-2} T - 9.095290 \times 10^{-3} T^2 + 1.001685 \times 10^{-4} T^3$$
$$-1.120083 \times 10^{-6} T^4 + 6.536332 \times 10^{-9} T^5$$
$$+ S(0.824493 - 4.0899 \times 10^{-3} T + 7.6438 \times 10^{-5} T^2 - 8.2467 \times 10^{-7} T^3 + 5.3875 \times 10^{-9} T^4)$$
$$+ S^{3/2}(-5.72466 \times 10^{-3} + 1.0227 \times 10^{-4} T - 1.6546 \times 10^{-6} T^2) + 4.8314 \times 10^{-4} S^2$$

The model equations are discretized into a finite-difference formulation on the staggered mesh grid C of Arakawa (Mesinger and Arakawa, 1976). The Grammeltvedt C scheme (Grammeltvedt, 1969), which conserves mass and total energy, is employed. For time integration, the Leapfrog scheme is used with an Euler scheme inserted at regular time intervals to eliminate the computational mode due to the central time differencing. For numerical stability, the frictional terms are lagged in time. The resulting finite difference forms of the momentum and continuity equations are:

$$\frac{U_{i,j}^{n+1} - U_{i,j}^{n-1}}{2\Delta t} = -\frac{1}{\Delta s}\left[\begin{array}{l} \frac{1}{2}\left(U_{i+1,j}^n + U_{i,j}^n\right)\times\frac{1}{2}\left\{\dfrac{U_{i+1,j}^n}{\frac{1}{2}\left(H_{i+2,j}^n + H_{i+1,j}^n\right)} + \dfrac{U_{i,j}^n}{\frac{1}{2}\left(H_{i+1,j}^n + H_{i,j}^n\right)}\right\} \\[4mm] -\frac{1}{2}\left(U_{i,j}^n + U_{i-1,j}^n\right)\times\frac{1}{2}\left\{\dfrac{U_{i,j}^n}{\frac{1}{2}\left(H_{i+1,j}^n + H_{i,j}^n\right)} + \dfrac{U_{i-1,j}^n}{\frac{1}{2}\left(H_{i,j}^n + H_{i-1,j}^n\right)}\right\} \end{array}\right]$$

$$-\frac{1}{\Delta s}\left[\begin{array}{l} \frac{1}{2}\left(V_{i+1,j}^n + V_{i,j}^n\right)\times\frac{1}{2}\left\{\dfrac{U_{i,j+1}^n}{\frac{1}{2}\left(H_{i+1,j+1}^n + H_{i,j+1}^n\right)} + \dfrac{U_{i,j}^n}{\frac{1}{2}\left(H_{i+1,j}^n + H_{i,j}^n\right)}\right\} \\[4mm] -\frac{1}{2}\left(V_{i+1,j-1}^n + V_{i,j-1}^n\right)\times\frac{1}{2}\left\{\dfrac{U_{i,j}^n}{\frac{1}{2}\left(H_{i+1,j}^n + H_{i,j}^n\right)} + \dfrac{U_{i,j-1}^n}{\frac{1}{2}\left(H_{i+1,j-1}^n + H_{i,j-1}^n\right)}\right\} \end{array}\right]$$

$$+ f\times\frac{1}{4}\left(V_{i+1,j}^n + V_{i+1,j-1}^n + V_{i,j}^n + V_{i,j-1}^n\right)$$

$$-\frac{g}{2}\left(H_{i+1,j}^n + H_{i,j}^n\right)\times\frac{1}{\Delta s}\left(H_{i+1,j}^n - H_{i,j}^n\right) - \frac{1}{2}g\left\{\frac{1}{2}\left(H_{i,j}^n + H_{i+1,j}^n\right)\right\}^2\frac{\rho_{i+1,j}^n - \rho_{i,j}^n}{\Delta s}$$

$$-\frac{g}{C^2}\times\left\{\dfrac{U_{i,j}^{n-1}}{\frac{1}{2}\left(H_{i,j}^{n-1} + H_{i+1,j}^{n-1}\right)}\right\}$$

$$\times\left[\left\{\dfrac{U_{i,j}^{n-1}}{\frac{1}{2}\left(H_{i,j}^{n-1} + H_{i+1,j}^{n-1}\right)}\right\}^2 + \left[\frac{1}{4}\left\{\dfrac{V_{i,j}^{n-1}}{\frac{1}{2}\left(H_{i,j}^{n-1} + H_{i,j-1}^{n-1}\right)} + \dfrac{V_{i+1,j}^{n-1}}{\frac{1}{2}\left(H_{i+1,j}^{n-1} + H_{i+1,j+1}^{n-1}\right)} + \dfrac{V_{i,j-1}^{n-1}}{\frac{1}{2}\left(H_{i,j-1}^{n-1} + H_{i,j}^{n-1}\right)} + \dfrac{V_{i+1,j-1}^{n-1}}{\frac{1}{2}\left(H_{i+1,j-1}^{n-1} + H_{i+1,j}^{n-1}\right)}\right\}\right]^2\right]^{1/2}$$

$$+\frac{\tau^x}{\rho}$$

$$+\frac{A}{(\Delta s)^2}\left(U_{i+1,j}^{n-1} + U_{i-1,j}^{n-1} + U_{i,j+1}^{n-1} + U_{i,j-1}^{n-1} - 4U_{i,j}^{n-1}\right)$$

$$\frac{V_{i,j}^{n+1} - V_{i,j}^{n-1}}{2\Delta t} = -\frac{1}{\Delta s}\left[\begin{array}{l}\frac{1}{2}\left(U_{i,j+1}^{n}+U_{i,j}^{n}\right)\times\frac{1}{2}\left\{\frac{V_{i+1,j}^{n}}{\frac{1}{2}\left(H_{i+1,j+1}^{n}+H_{i+1,j}^{n}\right)}+\frac{V_{i,j}^{n}}{\frac{1}{2}\left(H_{i,j+1}^{n}+H_{i,j}^{n}\right)}\right\}\\[3mm]-\frac{1}{2}\left(U_{i-1,j+1}^{n}+U_{i-1,j}^{n}\right)\times\frac{1}{2}\left\{\frac{V_{i,j}^{n}}{\frac{1}{2}\left(H_{i,j+1}^{n}+H_{i,j}^{n}\right)}+\frac{V_{i-1,j}^{n}}{\frac{1}{2}\left(H_{i-1,j+1}^{n}+H_{i-1,j}^{n}\right)}\right\}\end{array}\right]$$

$$-\frac{1}{\Delta s}\left[\begin{array}{l}\frac{1}{2}\left(V_{i,j+1}^{n}+V_{i,j}^{n}\right)\times\frac{1}{2}\left\{\frac{V_{i,j+1}^{n}}{\frac{1}{2}\left(H_{i,j+2}^{n}+H_{i,j+1}^{n}\right)}+\frac{V_{i,j}^{n}}{\frac{1}{2}\left(H_{i,j+1}^{n}+H_{i,j}^{n}\right)}\right\}\\[3mm]-\frac{1}{2}\left(V_{i,j}^{n}+V_{i,j-1}^{n}\right)\times\left\{\frac{V_{i,j}^{n}}{\frac{1}{2}\left(H_{i,j+1}^{n}+H_{i,j}^{n}\right)}+\frac{V_{i,j-1}^{n}}{\frac{1}{2}\left(H_{i,j}^{n}+H_{i,j-1}^{n}\right)}\right\}\end{array}\right]_{y}$$

$$-\frac{f}{4}\times\left(U_{i,j+1}^{n}+U_{i,j}^{n}+U_{i-1,j+1}^{n}+U_{i-1,j}^{n}\right)$$

$$-\frac{g}{2}\left(H_{i,j+1}^{n}+H_{i,j}^{n}\right)\times\frac{1}{\Delta s}\left(H_{i,j+1}^{n}-H_{i,j}^{n}\right)-\frac{1}{2}g\left\{\frac{1}{2}\left(H_{i,j}^{n}+H_{i,j+1}^{n}\right)\right\}^{2}\frac{\rho_{i,j+1}^{n}-\rho_{i,j}^{n}}{\Delta s}$$

$$-\frac{g}{C^{2}}\times\left\{\frac{V_{i,j}^{n-1}}{\frac{1}{2}\left(H_{i,j}^{n-1}+H_{i,j+1}^{n-1}\right)}\right\}$$

$$\times\left[\begin{array}{l}\left\{\frac{V_{i,j}^{n-1}}{\frac{1}{2}\left(H_{i,j}^{n-1}+H_{i,j+1}^{n-1}\right)}\right\}^{2}\\[3mm]+\left[\frac{1}{4}\left\{\frac{U_{i-1,j}^{n-1}}{\frac{1}{2}\left(H_{i-1,j}^{n-1}+H_{i-1,j+1}^{n-1}\right)}+\frac{U_{i,j}^{n-1}}{\frac{1}{2}\left(H_{i,j}^{n-1}+H_{i+1,j}^{n-1}\right)}+\frac{U_{i-1,j+1}^{n-1}}{\frac{1}{2}\left(H_{i-1,j+1}^{n-1}+H_{i,j+1}^{n-1}\right)}+\frac{U_{i,j+1}^{n-1}}{\frac{1}{2}\left(H_{i,j+1}^{n-1}+H_{i+1,j+1}^{n-1}\right)}\right\}\right]^{2}\end{array}\right]^{1/2}$$

$$+\frac{\tau}{\rho}$$

$$+\frac{A}{(\Delta s)^{2}}\left[V_{i+1,j}^{n-1}+V_{i-1,j}^{n-1}+V_{i,j+1}^{n-1}+V_{i,j-1}^{n-1}-4V_{i,j}^{n-1}\right]$$

$$\frac{H_{i,j}^{n+1} - H_{i,j}^{n-1}}{2\Delta t} = -\frac{1}{\Delta s}\left(U_{i,j}^{n} - U_{i-1,j}^{n}\right) - \frac{1}{\Delta s}\left(V_{i,j}^{n} - V_{i,j-1}^{n}\right)$$

where grid points are denoted as ith row and jth column, and the time step is denoted as nth time step.

2.3 Advection Scheme Used

For advective transport of salt and temperature, Hsu-Arakawa scheme, which was based on the Takacs scheme (1985), is adopted. In the following, first, a brief description of the Takacs scheme is presented, which is followed by a detailed description of the Hsu-Arakawa scheme and its application to the present model formulation.

TAKACS SCHEME

For simplicity, the formulation of the scheme will be based on the two-dimensional advection equation given by

$$\frac{\partial q}{\partial t} + u\frac{\partial q}{\partial x} + v\frac{\partial q}{\partial y} = 0 \tag{1}$$

Here, q represents any arbitrary quantity being advected, while u and v are velocity component of the flow in the x- and y-directions, respectively.

Following Takacs (1985), the two-dimensional scheme is derived by applying two passes of a one-dimensional operator. The one-dimensional operator was constructed by imposing three constraints on the time-continuous version of the scheme,

$$q_j^{n+1} = q_j^n - \frac{\mu}{2}\left(q_{j+1}^n - q_{j-1}^n\right) + \frac{\mu^2}{2}\left(q_{j+1}^n - 2q_j^n + q_{j-1}^n\right) - \alpha\mu(\mu-1)\left(q_{j+1}^n - 3q_j^n + 3q_{j-1}^n - q_{j-2}^n\right) \tag{2}$$

First, the requirement of conservation of mass was imposed yielding a flux formulation of the scheme,

$$\frac{\partial}{\partial t}\sum_j q_j = 0 . \tag{3}$$

Second, it was required that when the flow field is constant, the time-continuous flux form reduces to the time-continuous advective form given by

$$\frac{\partial q_j}{\partial t} = -\frac{u}{2\Delta x}\left(q_{j+1} - q_{j-1}\right) + \frac{\alpha u}{\Delta x}\left(q_{j+1} - 3q_j + 3q_{j-1} - q_{j-2}\right) \tag{4}$$

Finally, a stability criterion for the time-continuous case when the flow field is nondivergent was imposed, given by

$$\frac{\partial}{\partial t}\sum_j \frac{1}{2}q_j^2 \leq 0 . \tag{5}$$

Using these requirements, it can be shown that the flux form of (4) using a staggered grid is given by

$$\frac{\partial q_j}{\partial t} = -\frac{1}{2\Delta x}\left[u_j\left(q_{j+1} + q_j\right) - u_{j-1}\left(q_j + q_{j-1}\right)\right]$$

$$+\frac{\alpha}{\Delta x}\left[u_j\left(q_{j+1} - q_j\right) - \sqrt{u_j}\sqrt{u_{j-1}}\left(q_j - q_{j-1}\right) - u_{j-1}\left(q_j - q_{j-1}\right) + \sqrt{u_{j-1}}\sqrt{u_{j-2}}\left(q_{j-1} - q_{j-2}\right)\right]$$

For the time-discrete case ($\mu > 0$) and changing wind speeds, a predictor-corrector sequence can be devised which will reduce to Eq. (4) when the flow field is constant. Substitution will show that Eqs. (6) and (7) satisfy this requirement.

PREDICTOR:

$$q_j^* = q_j^n - \left[\mu_j q_j^n - \mu_{j-1} q_{j-1}^n\right] \tag{6}$$

CORRECTOR:

$$q_j^{n+1} = q_j^n - \frac{1}{2}\left[\mu_j\left(q_{j+1}^* + q_j\right) - \mu_{j-1}\left(q_j^* + q_{j-1}\right)\right]$$

$$+\frac{(1+\mu_j)}{6}\left[\mu_j\left(q_{j+1}^* - q_j^n\right) - \sqrt{\mu_j}\sqrt{\mu_{j-1}}\left(q_j^* - q_{j-1}^n\right)\right] \tag{7}$$

$$-\frac{(1+\mu_{j-1})}{6}\left[\mu_{j-1}\left(q_j^* - q_{j-1}^n\right) - \sqrt{\mu_{j-1}}\sqrt{\mu_{j-2}}\left(q_{j-1}^* - q_{j-2}^n\right)\right]$$

where $\mu_j = u_j \dfrac{\Delta t}{\Delta x}$.

Combining the predictor and corrector steps yields,

$$q_j^{n+1} = q_j^n - \frac{1}{2}\left[\mu_j\left(q_{j+1}^n - \mu_{j+1}q_{j+1}^n + \mu_j q_j^n + q_j^n\right) - \mu_{j-1}\left(q_j^n - \mu_j q_j^n + \mu_{j-1}q_{j-1}^n + q_{j-1}^n\right)\right]$$

$$+\frac{(1+\mu_j)}{6}\left[\mu_j\left(q_{j+1}^n - \mu_{j+1}q_{j+1}^n + \mu_j q_j^n - q_j^n\right) - \sqrt{\mu_j}\sqrt{\mu_{j-1}}\left(q_j^n - \mu_j q_j^n + \mu_{j-1}q_{j-1}^n - q_{j-1}^n\right)\right]$$

$$-\frac{(1+\mu_{j-1})}{6}\left[\mu_{j-1}\left(q_j^n - \mu_j q_j^n + \mu_{j-1}q_{j-1}^n - q_{j-1}^n\right) - \sqrt{\mu_{j-1}}\sqrt{\mu_{j-2}}\left(q_{j-1}^n - \mu_{j-1}q_{j-1}^n + \mu_{j-2}q_{j-2}^n - q_{j-2}^n\right)\right]$$

Nonpositive flow fields

In general, advection by a nonuniform two-dimensional flow requires additional information to ensure the inclusion of the proper grid-points for upstream-type schemes. A generalized form of the two-dimensional scheme for nonpositive flow is given by

PREDICTOR:

$$q_j^* = q_j^n - \left[F_j - F_{j-1}\right]$$

$$F_j = \mu_j^+ q_j^n + \mu_j^- q_{j+1}^n$$

where

$$\mu_j^+ = \left(\frac{\mu + |\mu|}{2}\right)_j$$

$$\mu_j^- = \left(\frac{\mu - |\mu|}{2}\right)_j$$

CORRECTOR:

$$q_j^{n+1} = q_j^n - \frac{1}{2}\left(P_j - P_{j-1}\right) + \left(\alpha_j Q_j - \alpha_{j-1} Q_{j-1}\right)$$

where

$$P_j = \mu_j^+\left(q_{j+1}^* + q_j^n\right) + \mu_j^-\left(q_j^* + q_{j+1}^n\right)$$

$$Q_j = \left[\mu_j^+\left(q_{j+1}^* - q_j^n\right) - \left(|\mu_j^+|\right)^{1/2}\left(|\mu_{j-1}^+|\right)^{1/2}\left(q_j^* - q_{j-1}^n\right)\right]$$
$$- \left[\mu_j^-\left(q_{j+1}^n - q_j^*\right) + \left(|\mu_j^-|\right)^{1/2}\left(|\mu_{j+1}^-|\right)^{1/2}\left(q_{j+2}^n - q_{j+1}^*\right)\right]$$

$$\alpha_j = \left(\frac{1+|\mu|}{6}\right)_j$$

Rewriting yields,

$$q_j^* = q_j^n - \left[\mu_j^+ q_j^n + \mu_j^- q_{j+1}^n - \mu_{j-1}^+ q_{j-1}^n - \mu_{j-1}^- q_j^n\right]$$

$$q_j^{n+1} = q_j^n - \frac{1}{2}\left[\mu_j^+\left(q_{j+1}^* + q_j^n\right) + \mu_j^-\left(q_j^* + q_{j+1}^n\right) - \mu_{j-1}^+\left(q_j^* + q_{j-1}^n\right) - \mu_{j-1}^-\left(q_{j-1}^* + q_j^n\right)\right]$$

$$+ \left(\frac{1+|\mu|}{6}\right)_j\left[\mu_j^+\left(q_{j+1}^* - q_j^n\right) - \left(|\mu_j^+|\right)^{1/2}\left(|\mu_{j-1}^+|\right)^{1/2}\left(q_j^* - q_{j-1}^n\right)\right]$$

$$- \left(\frac{1+|\mu|}{6}\right)_j\left[\mu_j^-\left(q_{j+1}^n - q_j^*\right) + \left(|\mu_j^-|\right)^{1/2}\left(|\mu_{j+1}^-|\right)^{1/2}\left(q_{j+2}^n - q_{j+1}^*\right)\right]$$

$$- \left(\frac{1+|\mu|}{6}\right)_{j-1}\left[\mu_{j-1}^+\left(q_j^* - q_{j-1}^n\right) - \left(|\mu_{j-1}^+|\right)^{1/2}\left(|\mu_{j-2}^+|\right)^{1/2}\left(q_{j-1}^* - q_{j-2}^n\right)\right]$$

$$+ \left(\frac{1+|\mu|}{6}\right)_{j-1}\left[\mu_{j-1}^-\left(q_j^n - q_{j-1}^*\right) + \left(|\mu_{j-1}^-|\right)^{1/2}\left(|\mu_j^-|\right)^{1/2}\left(q_{j+1}^n - q_j^*\right)\right]$$

HSU-ARAKAWA SCHEME

One of the drawbacks of the Takacs scheme is that it can generate negative values. Hsu and Arakawa (1990) developed an advection scheme based on the Takacs scheme, which is positive definite when time is continuous, while maintaining third-order accuracy when applied to a uniform current. In this scheme, the outflow flux from a grid point automatically approaches zero, while the inflow flux remains nonnegative. When applied to the one-dimensional advection equation with a uniform current, the results with this scheme are very similar to those from the Takacs scheme except that generation of negative values is practically eliminated. Horizontal discretization of the continuity equation in their model is based on this advection scheme.

Hsu-Arakawa scheme is based on the Arakawa C-grid, and consists of two steps (predictor and corrector steps) like the Takacs' scheme. The only differences come in the corrector step:

CORRECTOR:

$$q_j^{n+1} = q_j^n - \frac{\Delta t}{d}\left(F_j - F_{j-1}\right)$$

$$= q_j^n - \frac{\Delta t}{d}\left(u_j^+ \frac{q_{j+1}^* + q_j^n}{2} + u_j^- \frac{q_j^* + q_{j+1}^n}{2} + G_j - u_{j-1}^+ \frac{q_j^* + q_{j-1}^n}{2} - u_{j-1}^- \frac{q_{j-1}^* + q_j^n}{2} - G_{j-1}\right)$$

$$= q_j^n - \frac{1}{2}\left[\mu_j^+\left(q_{j+1}^* + q_j^n\right) + \mu_j^-\left(q_j^* + q_{j+1}^n\right) - \mu_{j-1}^+\left(q_j^* + q_{j-1}^n\right) - \mu_{j-1}^-\left(q_{j-1}^* + q_j^n\right)\right] - \frac{\Delta t}{d}\left(G_j + G_{j-1}\right)$$

$$= q_j^n - \frac{1}{2}\left[\mu_j^+\left(q_{j+1}^* + q_j^n\right) + \mu_j^-\left(q_j^* + q_{j+1}^n\right) - \mu_{j-1}^+\left(q_j^* + q_{j-1}^n\right) - \mu_{j-1}^-\left(q_{j-1}^* + q_j^n\right)\right]$$

$$+ \left(\frac{1+|\mu|}{6}\right)_j \begin{bmatrix} \mu_j^+\left\{1 + \left(\frac{1-2\alpha}{2\alpha}\right)_j \gamma_j^+\right\}\left(q_{j+1}^* - q_j^n\right) - \left(\mu_j^+ \mu_{j-1}^+\right)^{1/2}\left(1 - \hat{\gamma}_j^+\right)\left(q_j^* - q_{j-1}^n\right) \\ + \mu_j^-\left\{1 + \left(\frac{1-2\alpha}{2\alpha}\right)_j \gamma_j^-\right\}\left(q_j^* - q_{j+1}^n\right) - \left(\mu_j^- \|\mu_{j+1}^-\|\right)^{1/2}\left(1 - \hat{\gamma}_j^-\right)\left(q_{j+1}^* - q_{j+2}^n\right) \end{bmatrix}$$

$$- \left(\frac{1+|\mu|}{6}\right)_{j-1} \begin{bmatrix} \mu_{j-1}^+\left\{1 + \left(\frac{1-2\alpha}{2\alpha}\right)_{j-1} \gamma_{j-1}^+\right\}\left(q_j^* - q_{j-1}^n\right) - \left(\mu_{j-1}^+ \mu_{j-2}^+\right)^{1/2}\left(1 - \hat{\gamma}_{j-1}^+\right)\left(q_{j-1}^* - q_{j-2}^n\right) \\ + \mu_{j-1}^-\left\{1 + \left(\frac{1-2\alpha}{2\alpha}\right)_{j-1} \gamma_{j-1}^-\right\}\left(q_{j-1}^* - q_j^n\right) - \left(\mu_{j-1}^- \|\mu_j^-\|\right)^{1/2}\left(1 - \hat{\gamma}_{j-1}^-\right)\left(q_j^* - q_{j+1}^n\right) \end{bmatrix}$$

where

$$\gamma_j^+ = \overset{\wedge+}{\gamma}_j = \left[\frac{\left(q_{j-1}^n - 2q_j^n + q_{j+1}^n\right)^2}{\left(q_{j-1}^n - 2q_j^n + q_{j+1}^n\right) + q_j^n q_{j+1}^n} \right]^2$$

$$\gamma_j^- = \overset{\wedge-}{\gamma}_j = \left[\frac{\left(q_j^n - 2q_{j+1}^n + q_{j+2}^n\right)^2}{\left(q_j^n - 2q_{j+1}^n + q_{j+2}^n\right)^2 + q_j^n q_{j+1}^n} \right]^2$$

With these choices of γ and $\overset{\wedge}{\gamma}$, we can see that, as $q_j^n \to 0$, $F_j \to 0$ when $u_j > 0$ and

$F_{j-1} \to 0$ when $u_{j-1} < 0$. For other possibilities in choosing γ and $\overset{\wedge}{\gamma}$, see Hsu and Arakawa (1990).

It should be noted, in actual computations, one needs to make sure to set $\gamma_j^+ \to 0$,

$\overset{\wedge+}{\gamma}_j \to 0$, $\gamma_j^- \to 0$, and $\overset{\wedge-}{\gamma}_j \to 0$ as $q_j^n \to 0$.

In order to apply the Hsu-Arakawa scheme to a 2-D depth-integrated advection equation the following procedure is followed.
The 2-D depth-integrated equation for advection is given by

$$\frac{\partial HS}{\partial t} + \frac{\partial US}{\partial x} + \frac{\partial VS}{\partial y} = 0$$

where s is concentration of advected property (e. g., suspended sediment), $U = \int_{-h}^{\varsigma} u dz$,

$V = \int_{-h}^{\varsigma} v dz$, $S = \frac{1}{H} \int_{-h}^{\varsigma} s dz$, and $H = h + \varsigma$.

In order to apply the Hsu-Arakawa scheme to the above equation, it is necessary to account for volume changes into or out of the individual grid cells during each time-step, i. e., the following continuity equation needs to be solved at the same time,

$$\frac{\partial H}{\partial t} + \frac{\partial UH}{\partial x} + \frac{\partial VH}{\partial y} = 0$$

2.4 Model Application

Chandeleur-Breton Sound is situated immediately north of the Mississippi Delta (Figure 2-1). It is a relatively shallow estuary ranging from 3 to 6 m in depth, and is connected to an extensive wetland to the west. Previous attemps to model hydrodynamics in Breton Sound include that of Hart (1978) who utilized a depth-integrated two-dimensional hydrodynamic model based on the alternate-direction implicit model of Leendertse (1967). However, no previous model studies have addressed the issue of salinity distribution in Breton Sound including model verification in terms of simulated salinity distribution against observations.

The model bathymetry was based on the Nautical Charts (Scale 1:100,000). The model domain adopted is presented in Figure 2-2. A spatially uniform model grid size (between like variables) of 500 m was adopted. The model domain has three open boundaries along the northern, eastern and southern boundaries. Lack of tide stations near the open boundaries made it necessary to use existing tide stations within the model domain to estimate tidal heights along the open boundaries to force the model. For this model testing, no local wind forcing is assumed. The model was forced by predicted tides specified along the open boundaries and an artificial freshwater source is specified near Black Bay within Breton Sound, representing a local freshwater runoff. The time step used is 10 s, and the horizontal eddy viscosity chosen is $10 \ m^2 \ s^{-1}$. Initial testing included cases with the horizontal eddy diffusivities for temperature and salinity set to $10 \ m^2 \ s^{-1}$, $1 \ m^2 \ s^{-1}$, $0.1 \ m^2 \ s\text{-}1$, and $0.001 \ m^2 \ s^{-1}$. The model has been proven to be stable even for zero diffusivities. For the results shown in Figures 2-3a through 2-3c, the horizontal eddy diffusivities of $10 \ m^2 \ s^{-1}$ were used for both temperature and salinity. The initial conditions were that salinities everywhere in the model domain were set to 35 psu. A freshwater discharge of $1,000 \ m^3 \ s^{-1}$ was turned on at Day 0, and it was kept at that flow rate continuously while the model was run for three months forced by the incoming tides (estimated based on predicted tides in the neighboring tidal stations in the area) specified at the open boundaries. As the time integration proceeds, the size of the freshwater plume emanating from the freshwater source gradually expands. At Day 30, the 34 psu contour is toward the outer edges of Breton Sound while the steepest salinity gradient can be found closer to the source. At Day 60, the 34 psu contour reaches the outer edges of Chandeleur-Breton Sound. At Day 90, filling of Chandeleur-Breton Sound with fresher water plume continues, though there are small pockets of higher salinity water trapped near the coast. It is interesting to note that the evolving salinity field simulated in the model resembles to some of the observed salinity distributions shown in Figures 2-4a and 2-4b previously reported by Geaghan (1995). Estimated differences between the post- and pre-diversion are shown in Figure 2-4c.

A freshwater diversion at Caernarvon became operational in January 1991 to divert freshwater from the Mississippi River in order to control salinity distribution in Breton Sound. Flow rate at the freshwater diversion was controlled and measured since then (shown in Figure 2-5). In order to assess the impact of the freshwater diversion on salinity distribution in Breton Sound, Geaghan (1995) carried out a statistical analysis to determine if there were any detectable

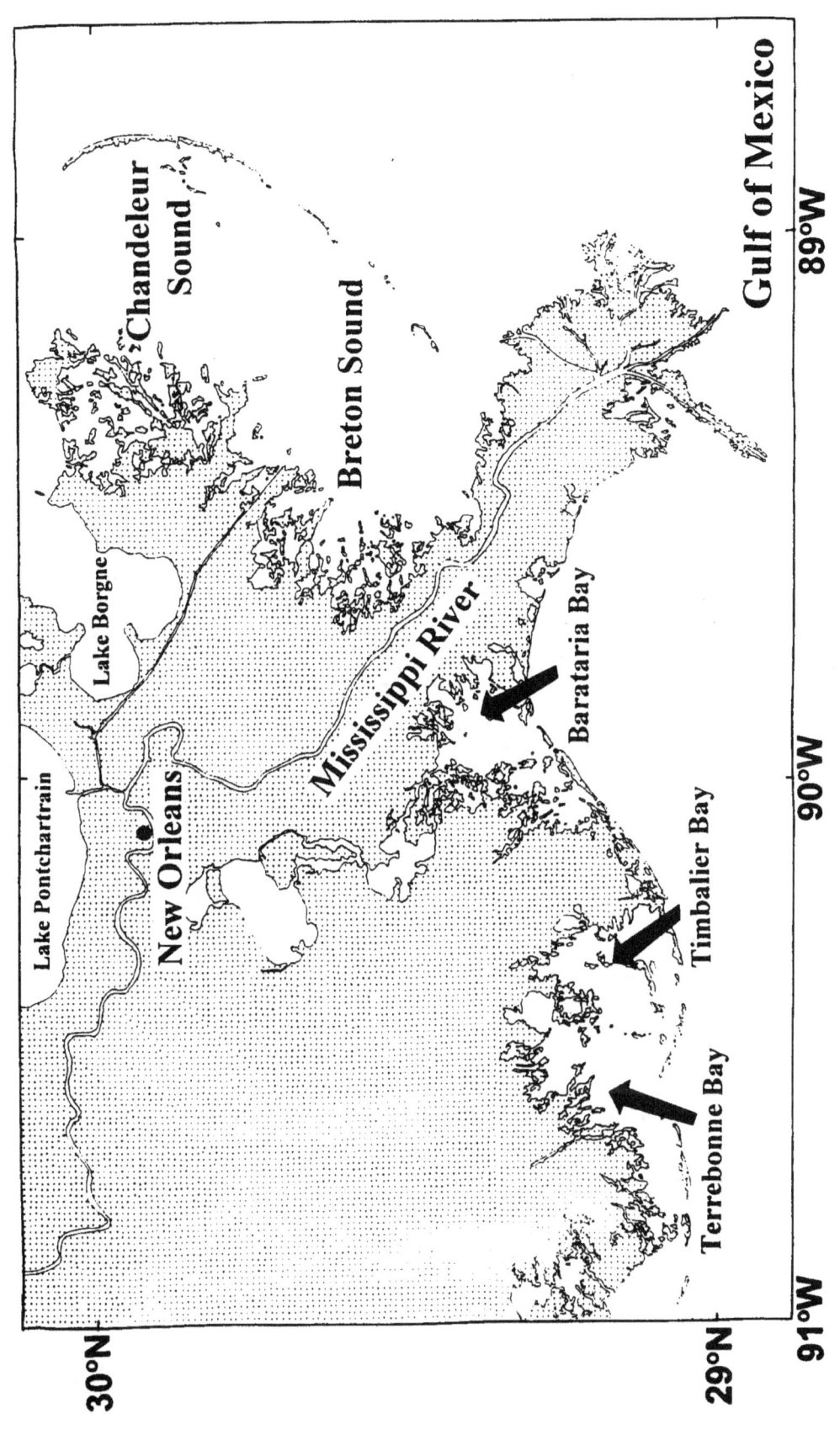

Figure 2-1 Map of study area showing Chandeleur-Breton Sound located just north of the Mississippi Delta.

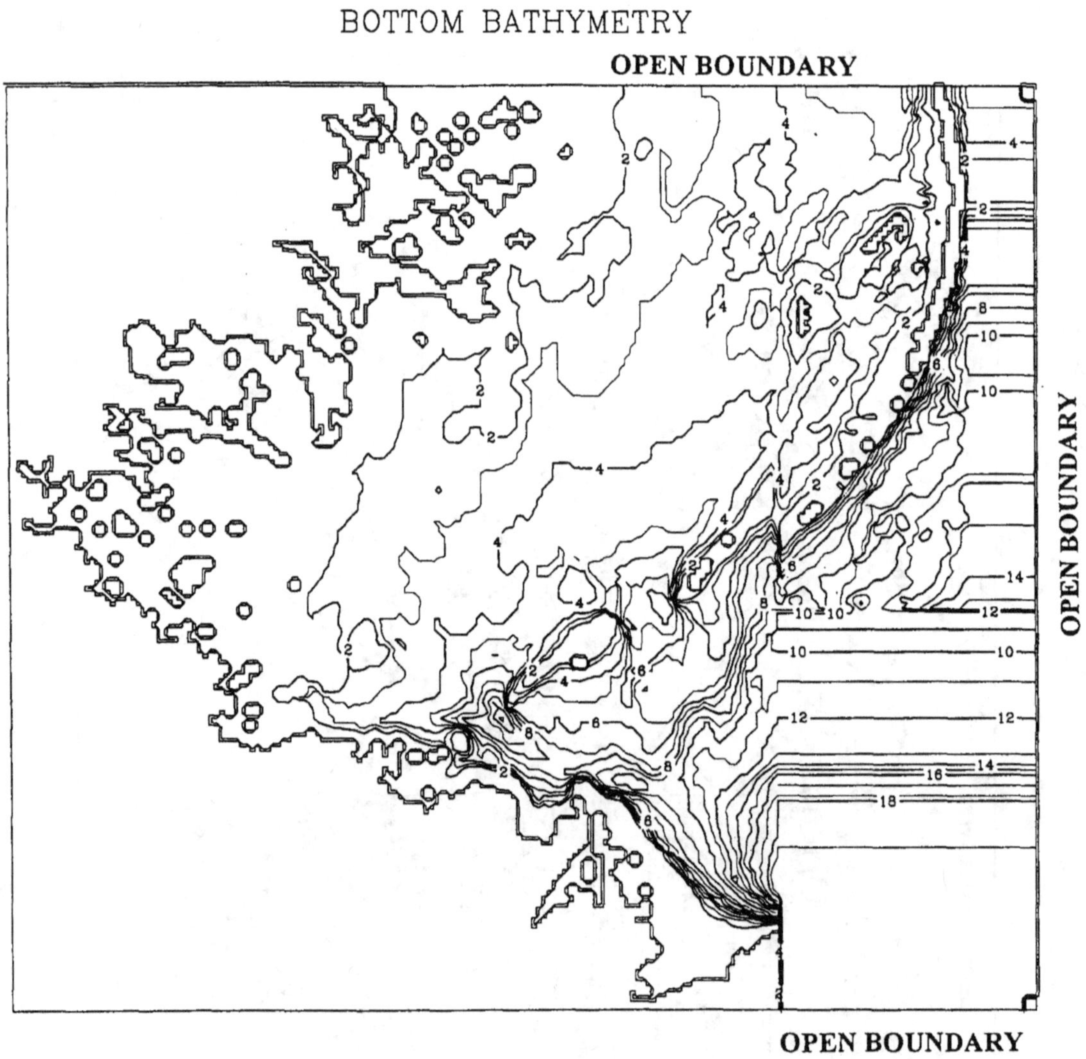

BOTTOM BATHYMETRY

Figure 2-2. Model domain of the Chandeleur/Breton Sound Model. There are three open boundaries located along the northern, eastern, and southern boundaries. Bottom bathymetric contours are shown at every meter. Extrapolated values are used for the bottom contours outside the Breton Sound. There are 200 grids in X-axis and 178 grids in Y-axis with grid size of 500 m.

SALINITY (DAY 30)

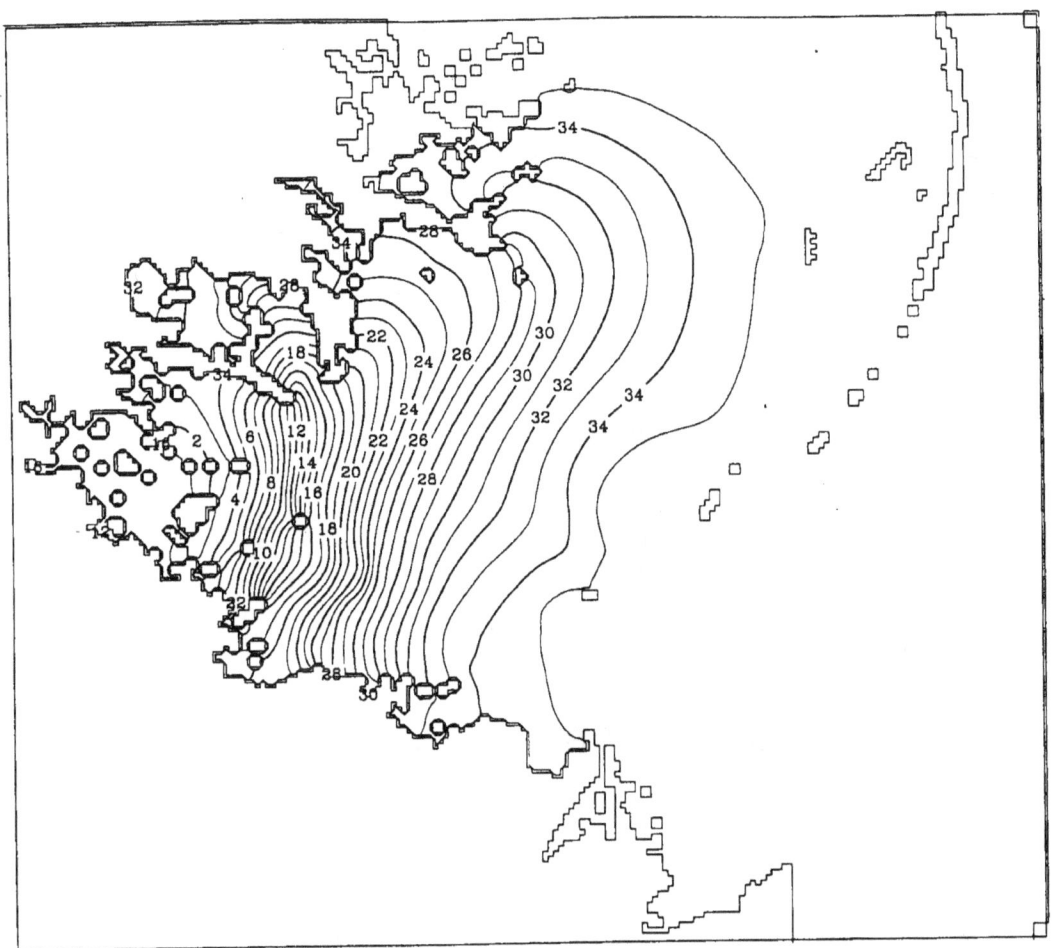

Figure 2-3a. Simulated salinity distribution at Day 30. A freshwater discharge of 1,000 m³ s⁻¹ is turned on at Day 0 at the head of the estuary, and kept at that flow rate continuously.

SALINITY (DAY 60)

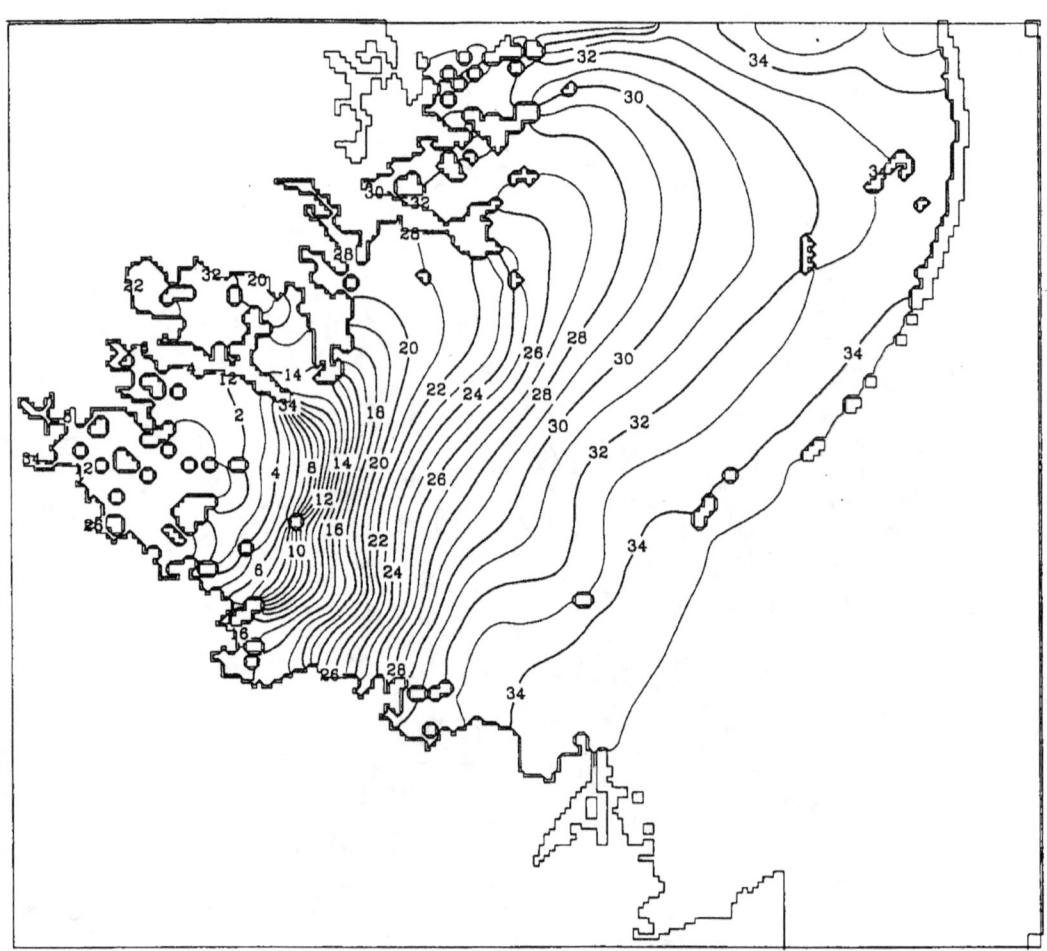

Figure 2-3b. Distribution of simulated salinity at Day 60.

SALINITY (DAY 90)

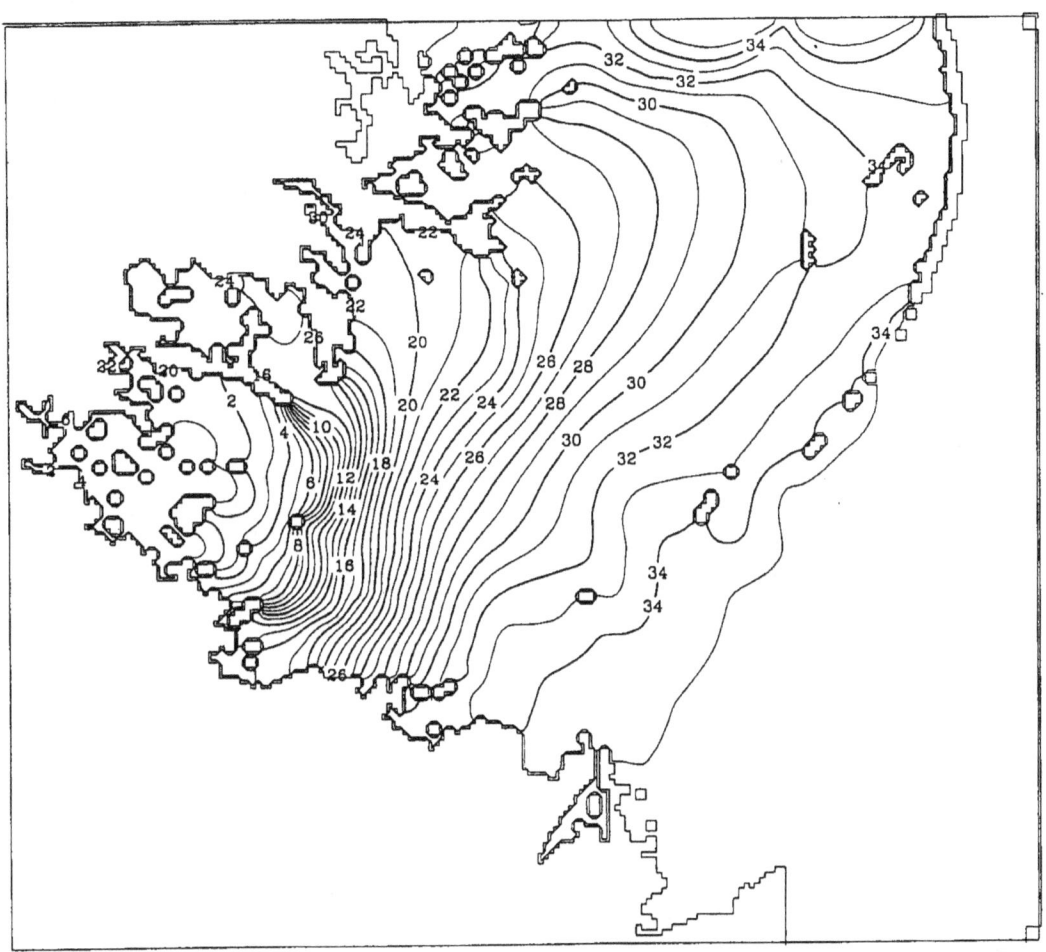

Figure 2-3c. Distribution of simulated salinity at Day 90.

SALINITY (PRE−DIVERSION)

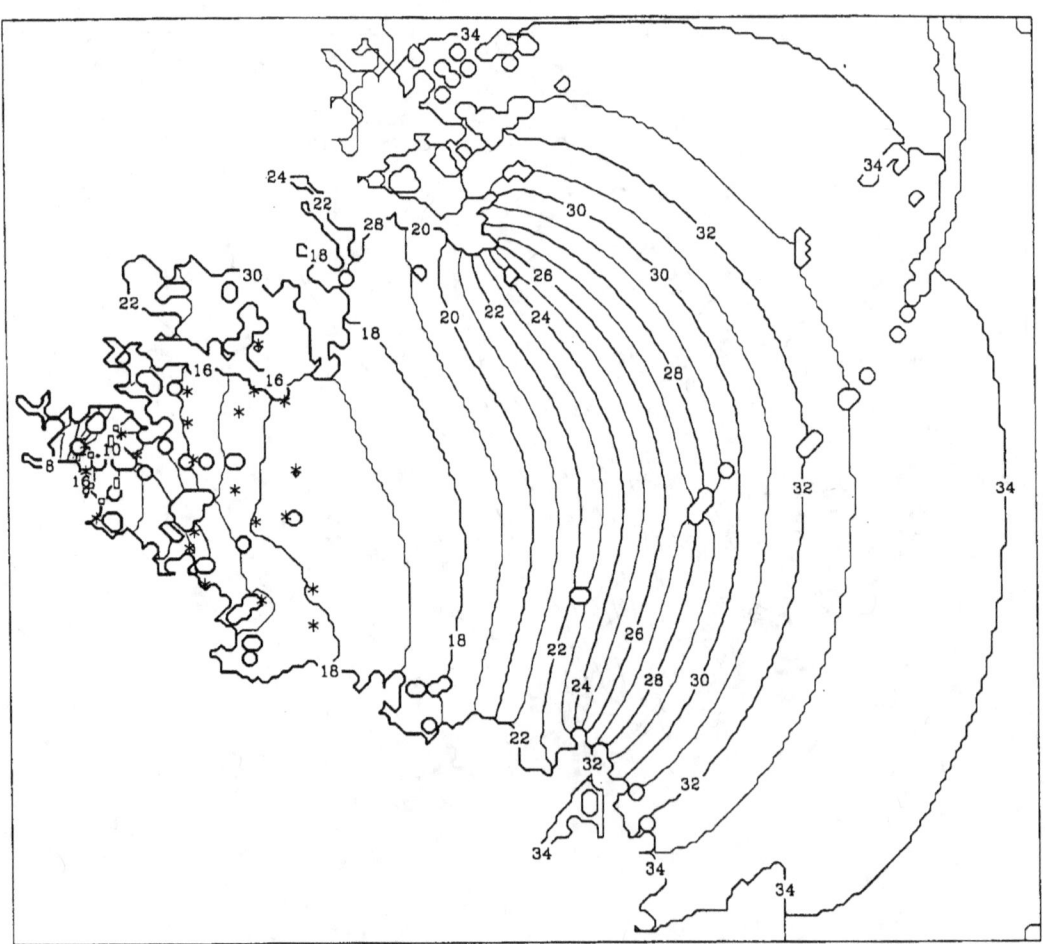

Figure 2-4a. Estimated pre-diversion salinity distribution prior to the opening of Caernarvon
freshwater diversion structure. Asterisks indicate the locations of actual salinity
observations reported in Geaghan (1995). Note that all the observations were
made only in the upstream region of the model domain, and an extrapolation
was used outside the observed region. Observed values are based on mean of
monthly observations collected for the period 1988-1990.

SALINITY (POST-DIVERSION)

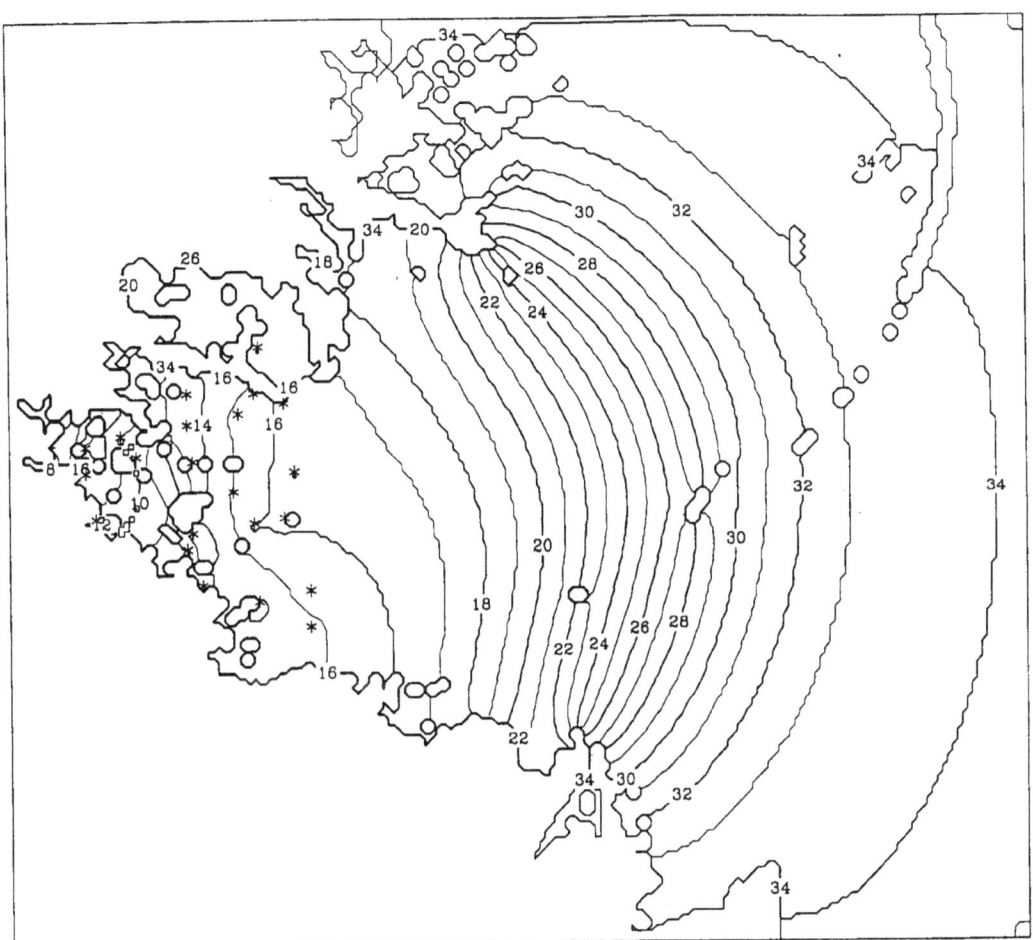

Figure 2-4b. Estimated post-diversion salinity distribution after the opening of Caernarvon freshwater diversion structure. Asterisks indicate the locations of actual salinity observations reported in Geaghan (1995). Note that all the observations were made only in the upstream region of the model domain, and an extrapolation was used outside the observed region. Observed values are based on mean of monthly observations collected for the period 1991-1994.

34

SALINITY (Difference)

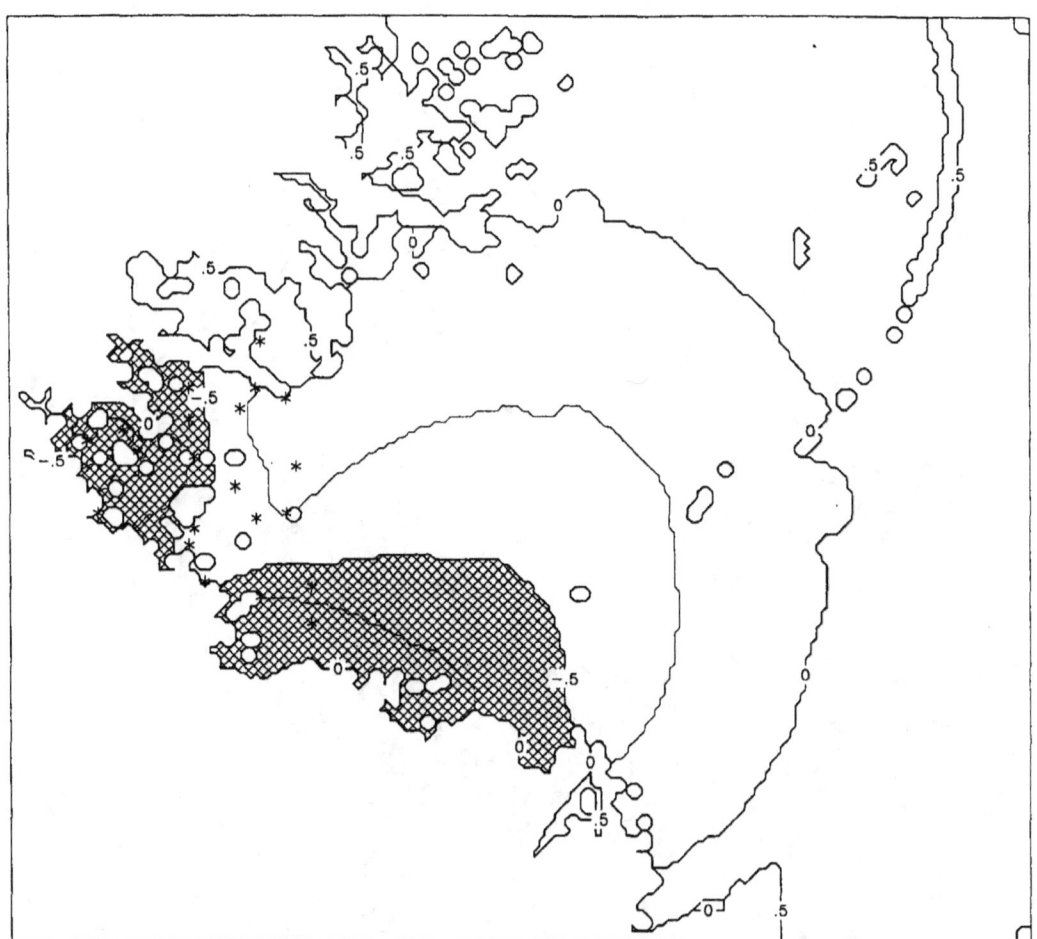

Figure 2-4c. Estimated differences (post – pre) in salinity distribution due to the opening of
Caernarvon freshwater diversion structure, i. e., Figure 2-4b minus Figure 2-4a.
Contours shown are at every 0.25 psu. Shaded regions have values < -0.5 psu.
Asterisks indicate the locations of actual salinity observations reported in Geaghan
(1995). Note that all the observations are limited to the upstream region of the
model domain, and an extrapolation is used outside the observed region.

pre-diversion versus post-diversion operation effects. Figure 2-4a shows the pre-diversion salinity distribution, and the post-diversion distribution is presented in Figure 2-4b. It should be noted that Figures 2-4a and 2-4b are based on salinity measurements made at 22 discrete measurement stations located only in the upstream region of the model domain. Moreover, salinity measurements were made at monthly intervals between 1988 and 1994. Measurements prior to January 1991 were grouped into mean values representing pre-diversion values, and the period between August 1991 through 1994 were treated as post-diversion values (Geaghan, 1995). To highlight the differences between the pre- and post-diversion salinity distributions, Figure 2-4b minus Figure 2-4a is presented in Figure 2-4c. The overall impact of Caernarvon diversion is to freshen local salinities by 0.5~0.75 psu in the upper region of the domain. Unfortunately, the question of how far this freshening impact might have extended outside the region actually measured, can not be answered.

An attempt was made to use the hydrodynamic model to simulate salinity changes due to the freshwater diversion. For this simulation, pre-diversion salinity distribution was used as the initial condition for the model, representing the salinity distribution in January 1, 1991. The freshwater diversion was represented as two separate sources of freshwater runoff representing Bayou Terreaux Boeufs and River aux Chenes. Flow rate for the freshwater diversion was varied according to the diversion flow rate actually measured for the period January 1991-August 1991 (see Figure 2-5). Although the total flow rate at Caernarvon was measured, how this was split between the two outlets, namely Bayou Terreaux Boeufs and River aux Chenes, is not known. Therefore, for this simulation, it was decided to split the total flow rate into 25% for Bayou Terreaux Boeufs and 75% for River aux Chenes. The diversion was turned on at time t=0, corresponding to January 1, 1991, and the hydrodynamic model was integrated for eight months forced by the predicted tides and actual freshwater diversion flow rate. The computed salinity after eight months was considered to represent computed post-diversion salinity distribution.

A major unknown factor is the background freshwater runoff from the surrounding drainage basin, that presumably gave rise to the observed pre-diversion salinity distribution shown in Fig. 2-4a. Additionally, this background runoff could have varied significantly in time and presumably in space. In order to simplify the simulation strategy, we decided not to specify the background freshwater runoff. The resulting salinity distribution from this diversion simulation includes not only the impact of freshwater diversion but also the impact of run-down salinity distribution due to the neglect of local background runoff. In order to highlight the true impact of diversion, a reference simulation was carried out where no freshwater diversion was specified while everything else remained the same, i. e., the initial salinity distribution was allowed to run-down due to tidal mixing. The, output from the diversion simulation was contrasted to the reference salinity distribution based on the reference simulation. Figure 2-6a shows the impact of diversion after two months of model simulation. Compared to Figure 2-4c, salinities are lower near the two diversion outlets though the spatial pattern is similar. After eight months of model simulation (Figure 2-6b), an expanding fresher water plume in the upper region of the domain is quite fresher than the observations shown in Figure 2-4c. It is noted that an extensive extrapolation is used in deriving those figures, therefore, it is more meaningful to

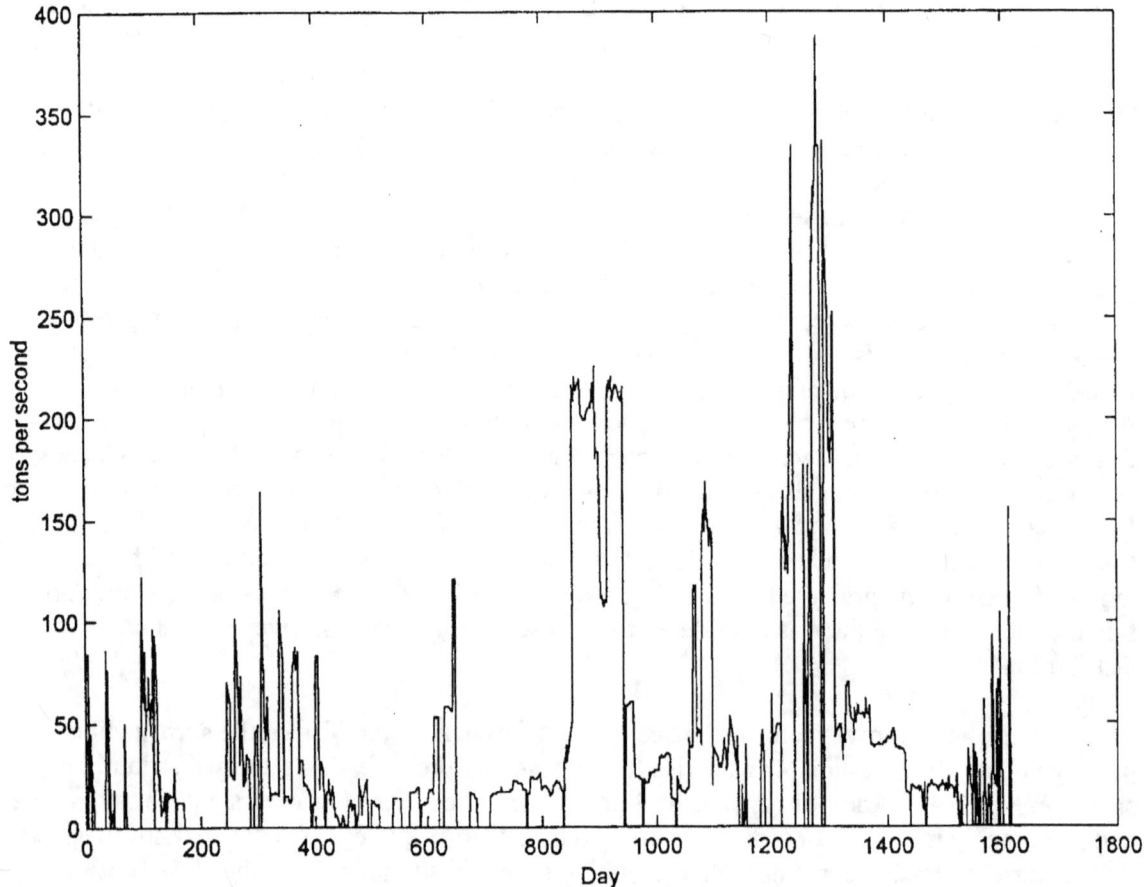

Figure 2-5. Measured freshwater diversion flow rate at Caernarvon. Time origin is January 1, 1991 (Enrique Reyes, personal communication, 2001).

SALINITY (Difference)

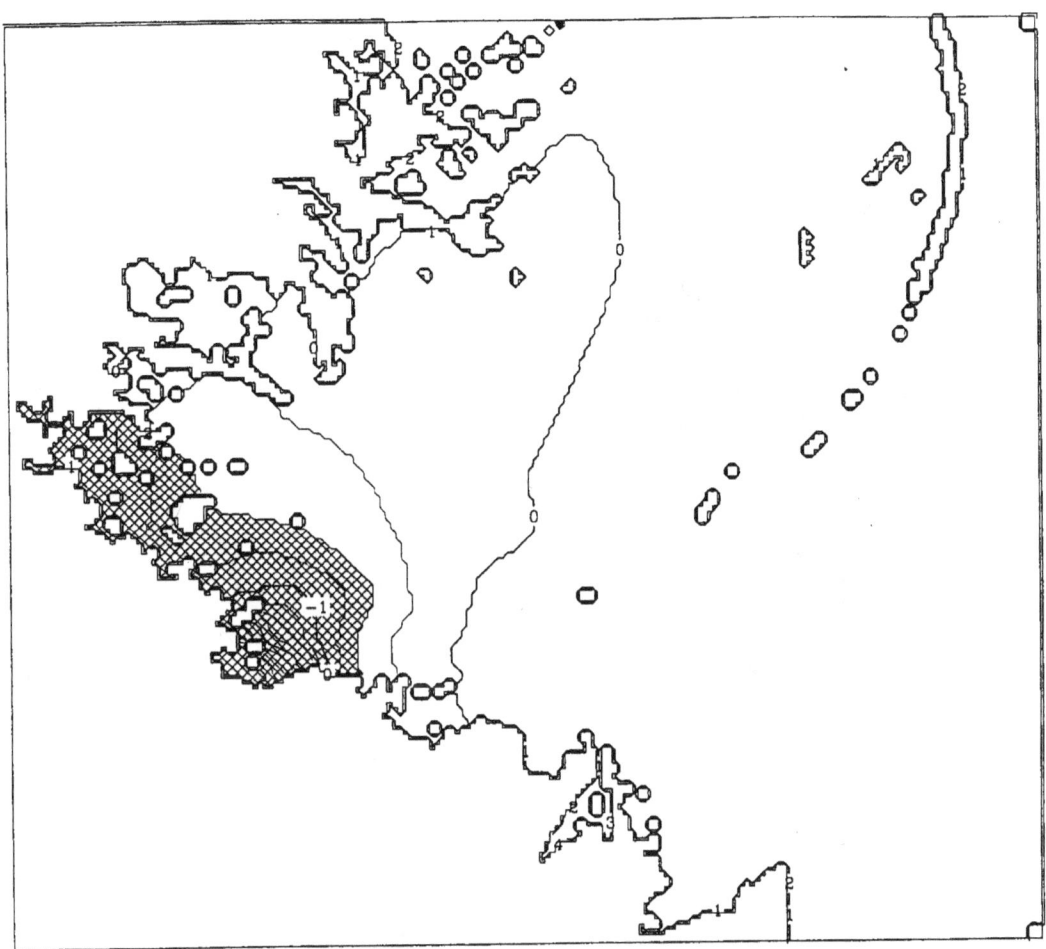

Figure 2-6a. Computed impact of Caernarvon diversion after two months. Differences between
the diversion simulation and the reference simulation. Contours shown are at every
0.25 psu. Shaded regions have values < -0.5 psu.

38

SALINITY (Difference)

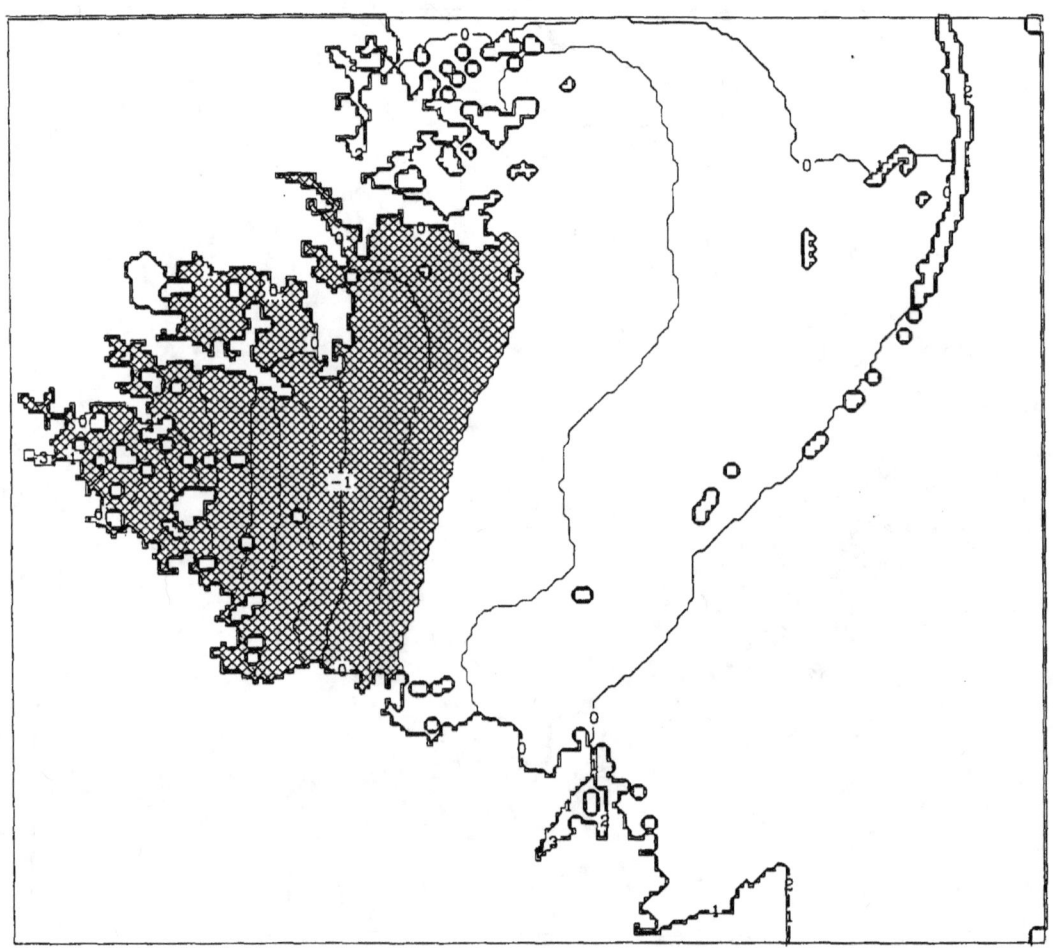

Figure 2-6b. Computed impact of Caernarvon diversion after eight months. Differences
between the diversion simulation and the reference simulation. Contours shown
are at every 0.25 psu. Shaded regions have values < -0.5 psu.

compute spatial correlation (r-square values) between the computed diversion impact and the observed diversion impact based only on the 17 measurement stations shown in Figure 2-4c. R-square value increases gradually from 0.475 in month 1, to 0.772 in month 6, and then decreases to 0.592 in month 8. Mean value of computed diversion impact at 17 measurement stations gradually increases from –0.29 psu in month 1 to –2.36 psu in month 8. Those values are to be contrasted to the observed mean of –0.65 psu for the post-diversion condition. It appears that the computed diversion impact shows too much fresh water accumulation in the upper region of the domain, while the computed spatial pattern is in general agreement with the observed impact. A possible reason for this discrepancy could be variations in the background freshwater runoff from the surrounding drainage basin that was not accounted for in the simulation. Interestingly, based on a purely statistical analysis, Geaghan (1995) came to a conclusion that the observed impact of Caernarvon diversion appears to be limited, and suggested a possible impact due to variations in the nearby Mississippi River discharge.

Other possible reasons for the observed discrepancy could be (1) impact of wind over the shelf as well as local wind, not accounted for in the simulation; (2) classification into pre- and post-diversion types might be too simplistic. Ideally, interannual simulation accounting for local runoff, as well as freshwater diversion, plus wind forcing needs to be carried out in order to fully assess the usefulness of the hydrodynamic model.

2.5 Summary

The two-dimensional depth-integrated hydrodynamic model previously developed and applied to the estuaries in Louisiana, has been enhanced by including baroclinic pressure gradient. An accurate advection scheme, namely the Hsu-Arakawa scheme, has been adopted to compute advection of temperature and salinity. The model was applied to Chandeleur-Breton Sound to simulate salinity distribution.

CHAPTER 3

PRELIMINARY RESULTS FROM FIELD DEPLOYMENT

3.1 Introduction

One of the ultimate goals of these modeling studies is the ability to predict sediment transport within the coastal bays of Louisiana. In an effort to begin to understand the importance of the various processes responsible for such sediment transport, we deployed a bottom-mounted system within Terrebonne Bay (Figure 3-1) for two summer periods.

The measurement system was deployed in water depth of approximately 2 m, and sampled bottom pressure, current at three levels, and optical backscatter at three levels, corresponding to 30 cm, 68 cm and 109 cm above the bottom. Samples were collected at 4 Hertz for 8.5 minutes each hour. This provided 2040 samples each hour for Fourier analysis. The current meters were Marsh-McBirney electro-magnetic current meters deployed to sample horizontal flows. The optical backscatter sensors had been deployed in various bays at other times, largely during the spring runoff period and the fall stormy season. They were calibrated for the dynamic range experienced during these previous deployments. This proved to be far too broad for summertime conditions. Also, previous experience indicated that the optics degraded rapidly because of buildup of material on the lenses of the sensors. Historically, cleaning these lenses every three or four days had proven to be sufficient to allow recording of good data. During the present summertime deployments, this maintenance schedule proved to be inadequate. At best, qualitative data was collected. The records clearly indicated a drift of the sensors during periods between cleansing of the lenses and abrupt alterations of the measured values immediately after cleansing. In order to improve the data available, we have ordered transmissometers, which are compatible with the recording systems we are using, from an Australian company. These transmissometers are equipped with wiper blades that will clean the lenses of the sensors at a far more frequent rate than is practical using field personnel. As soon as these arrive, they will be installed in the measurement system and the system will be redeployed to obtain quantitative data. These data will then be compared with various simple models of sediment resuspension and transport in order to determine which model should be incorporated into the code of our bay model.

3.2 Observations

The two summertime observation periods, 7/21/98-8/21/98 and 7/30/99-9/24/99, produced similar results. In both cases the measured flow fields, at periods of hours and longer, were dominated by the tidal current signal. Characteristic speeds during tropic tidal conditions were in excess of 40 cm/s and occasionally exceeded 70 cm/s (Figure 3-2). The long term mean speeds exhibited a characteristic frictional decay with depth as is to be expected in such shallow, tidally-dominated environments. The velocities appeared to be bathymetrically-steered. Such a situation was previously observed in Terrebonne Bay (Wiseman and Inoue, 1994). While prior observations over a year-long deployment indicate that the subtidal current directions are

42

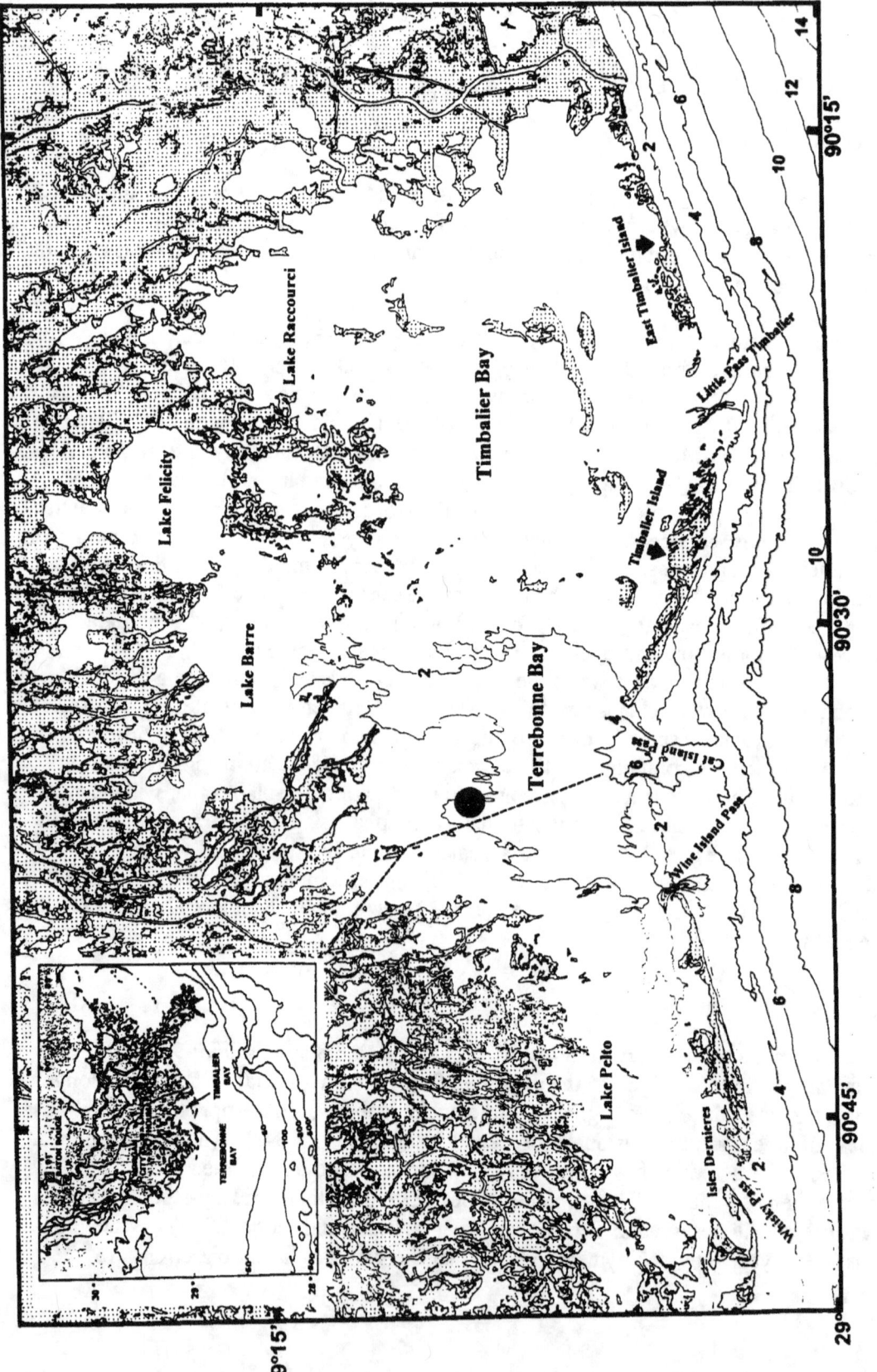

Figure 3-1. Chart of Terrebonne Bay indicating location of mooring deployments (solid circle). Bottom bathymetric contours are shown at every 2 m.

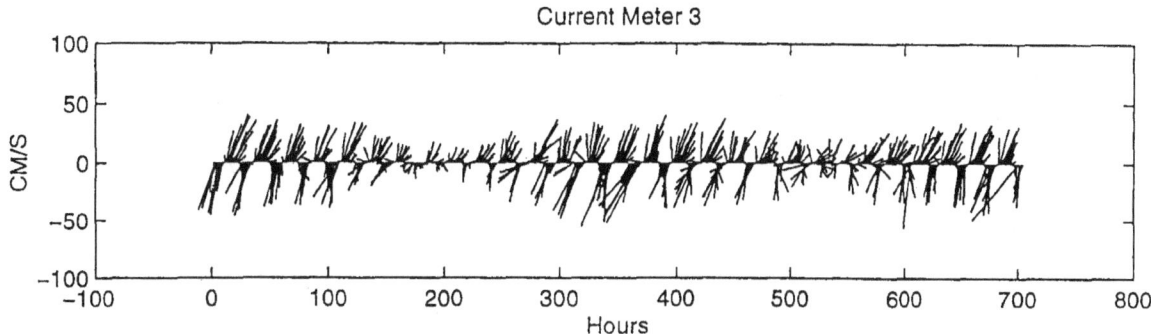

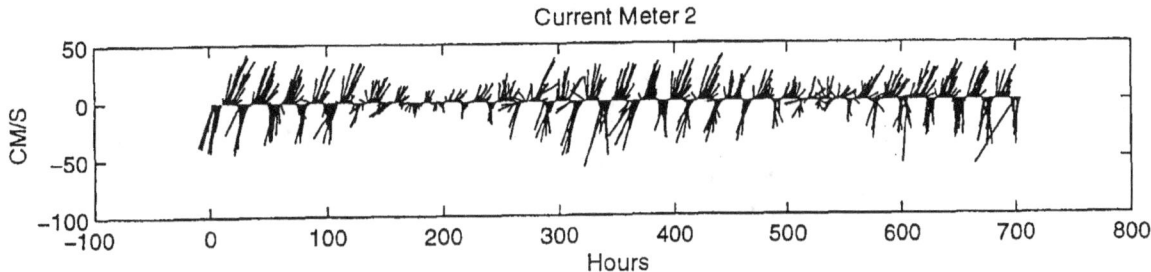

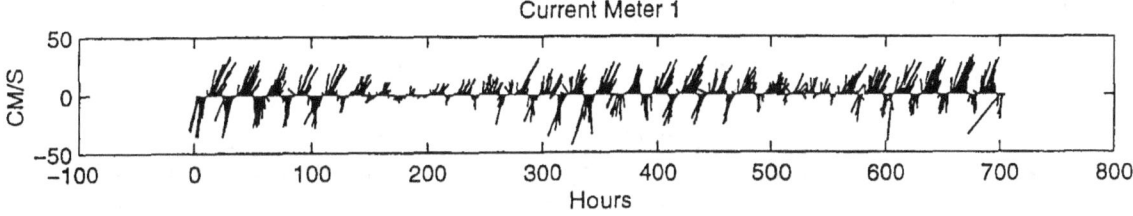

Figure 3.2. Stickplots of currents measured at three levels (30 cm, 68 cm and 109 cm) off the bottom (bottom depth of approximately 2m) at one site during the second deployment. Note the dominance of the tidal currents. North is upward. Time origin is July 30, 1999.

dictated by the winds, these summer deployments were too short and winds were too weak to allow definitive corroboration of these earlier results.

Bottom pressure records often indicated the presence of a surface gravity wave field with characteristic periods of 2.5 to 3 seconds. These typical, locally wind-generated waves were more clearly depicted, though, in the bottom current records. Root mean square currents about the hourly means were typically 5 – 10 cm/s. Maximum amplitudes appeared to occur with a diurnal periodicity. It is not yet clear whether this is due to the sea breeze cycle or the tidal cycle. Occasionally, the period of peak wave energy shifted to lower values approaching 7 seconds, values more characteristic of swell in the open Gulf of Mexico than of wind waves locally-generated within the Bay (Figure 3-3). This suggests that periods such as hour 300 (Figure 3-3 a,b) are indicative of locally wind-generated wave action, while periods such as hour 100 (Figure 3-3 c,d) are indicative of far-field wave generation. Indeed, winds from the local C-MAN station at Grand Isle indicate the presence of weak southerly coastal winds during hour 100 with stronger northeasterly coastal winds during hour 300 (Figure 3-4). In these cases, the waves enter the Bay through the broad, deep Cat Island Pass (Figure 3-1).

It is interesting to note that the waves during the high frequency events, e.g. hour 300, are associated with stronger near-bottom currents. Indeed, although the optical backscatter sensors did not provide quantitatively useful data, they did indicate qualitatively that resuspension was more important during the strongly forced high-frequency events than during the weaker events when oceanic swell was dominant.

3.3 Conclusions

Preliminary results from the initial deployments have been presented. Additional analysis of the data will be needed to examine and resolve locally-generated wind waves and swell. It is clear from these isolated and incomplete measurements that wave-induced sediment resuspension is an important and poorly understood process within the shallow coastal bays of Louisiana's Gulf coast. Of particular interest will be the importance of oceanic swell during pre-frontal winter conditions in resuspending bay bottom sediments. We anticipate that our next deployments will better characterize these processes and allow us to select a resuspension model, (e. g., Luettich et al., 1990; Smith, 1977; Grant and Madsen, 1979) adequate for incorporation into our modeling framework.

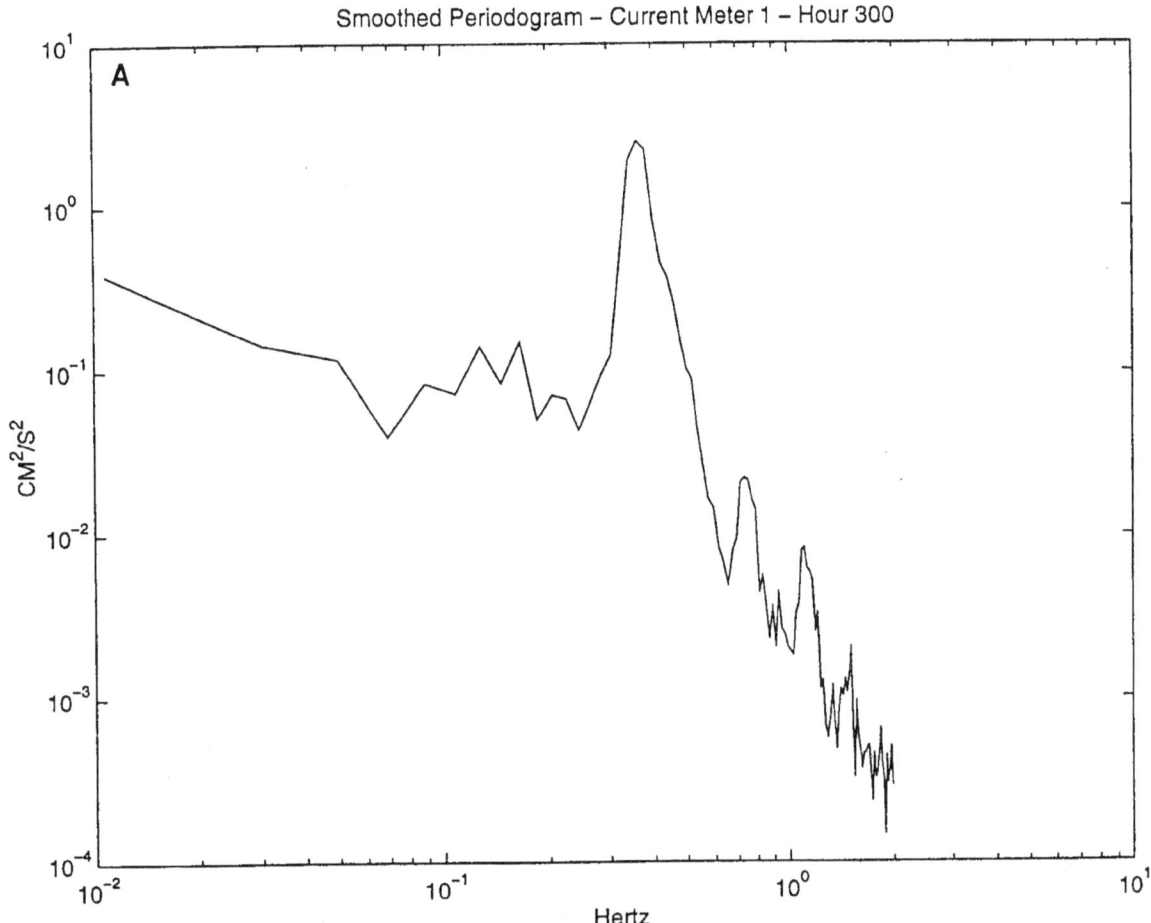

Figure 3-3. Spectra of a) near bottom currents around hour 300, b) near-bottom pressure variance around hour 300, c) near bottom currents around hour 100, and d) near-bottom pressure variance around hour 100. Pressure variance is in arbitrary (but the same) units in subplots b and d. Note the dominance of the 2.5 to 3 second waves around hour 300 while much longer periods dominate around hour 100. Note, also, the more energetic motions near hour 300.

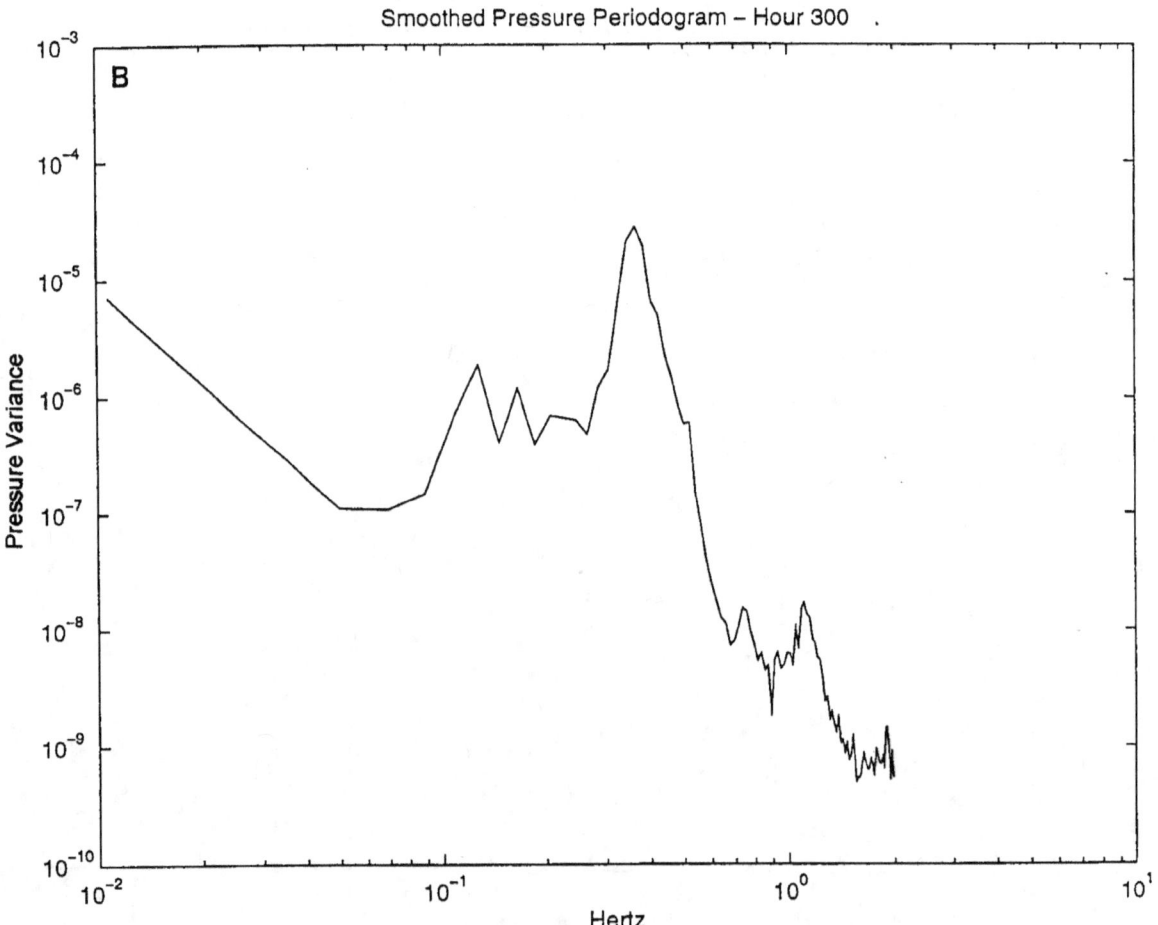

Figure 3-3. Spectra of a) near bottom currents around hour 300, b) near-bottom pressure variance around hour 300, c) near bottom currents around hour 100, and d) near-bottom pressure variance around hour 100. Pressure variance is in arbitrary (but the same) units in subplots b and d. Note the dominance of the 2.5 to 3 second waves around hour 300 while much longer periods dominate around hour 100. Note, also, the more energetic motions near hour 300.

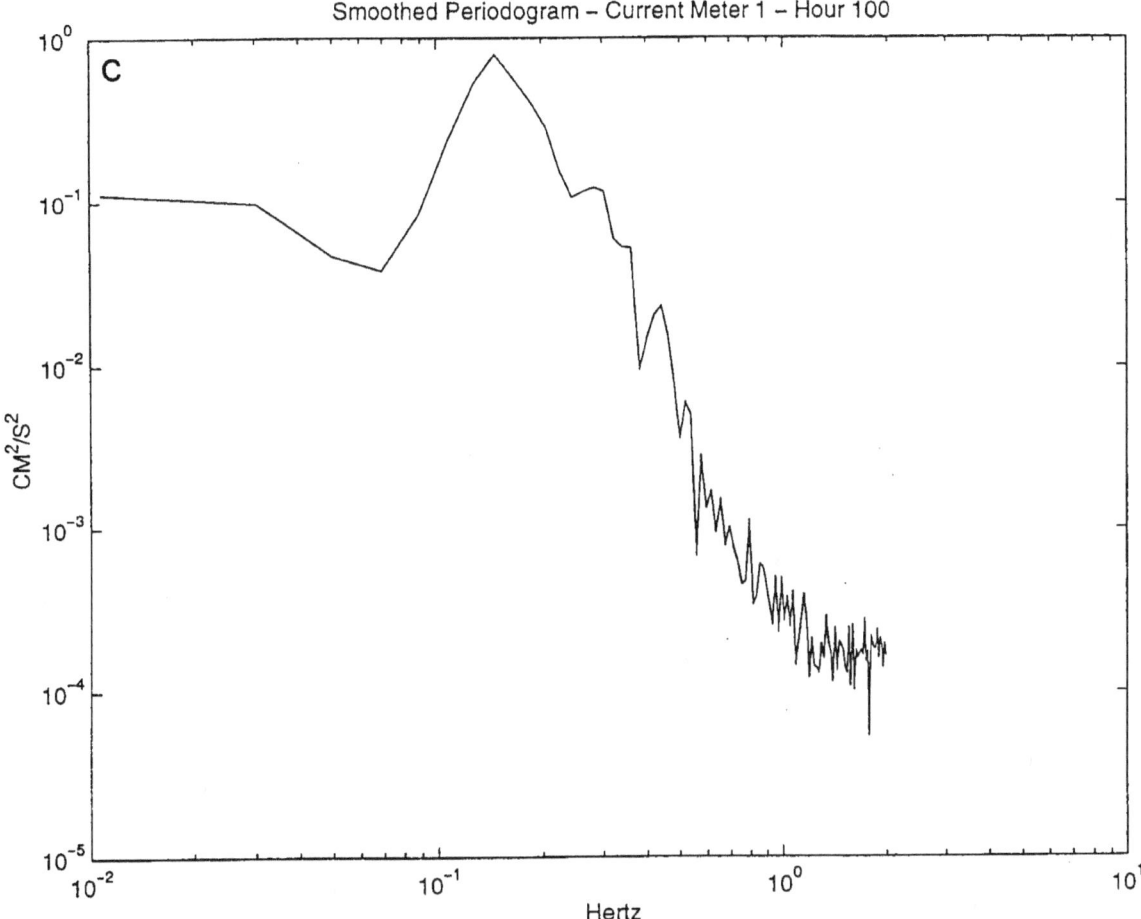

Figure 3-3. Spectra of a) near bottom currents around hour 300, b) near-bottom pressure variance around hour 300, c) near bottom currents around hour 100, and d) near-bottom pressure variance around hour 100. Pressure variance is in arbitrary (but the same) units in subplots b and d. Note the dominance of the 2.5 to 3 second waves around hour 300 while much longer periods dominate around hour 100. Note, also, the more energetic motions near hour 300.

48

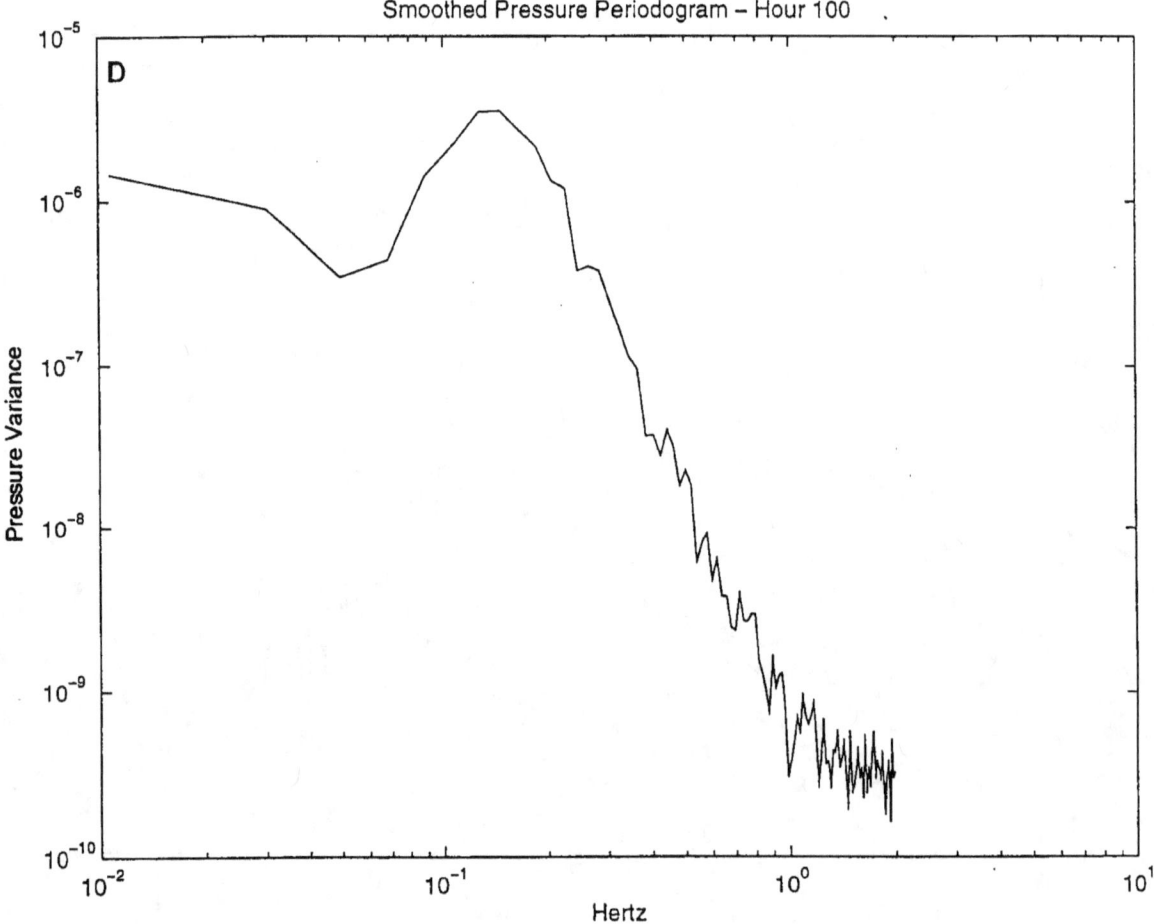

Figure 3-3. Spectra of a) near bottom currents around hour 300, b) near-bottom pressure variance around hour 300, c) near bottom currents around hour 100, and d) near-bottom pressure variance around hour 100. Pressure variance is in arbitrary (but the same) units in subplots b and d. Note the dominance of the 2.5 to 3 second waves around hour 300 while much longer periods dominate around hour 100. Note, also, the more energetic motions near hour 300.

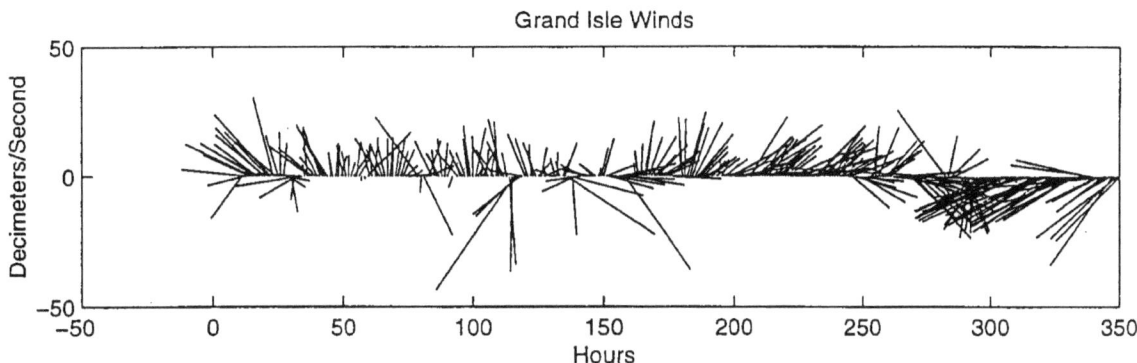

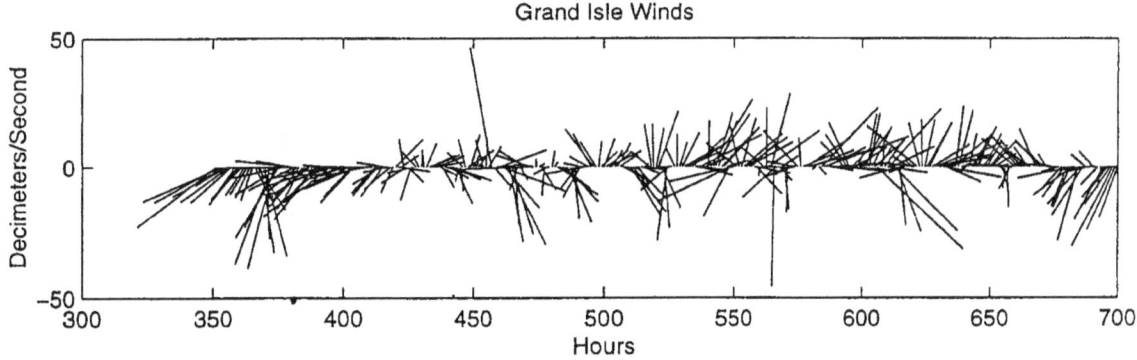

Figure 3-4. Stickplot of winds measured at the Grand Isle C-MAN station during the second deployment. North is upward. Time origin is July 30, 1999.

REFERENCES

Awaji, T. 1982. Water mixing in a tidal current and the effect of turbulence on tidal exchange through a strait. J. Phys. Oceanogr. **12**, 501-514.

Awaji, T., N. Imasato, and H. Kunishi. 1980. Tidal exchange through a strait: A numerical experiment using a simple model basin. J. Phys. Oceanogr. **10**, 1449-1508.

Banas, P. J. 1978. An investigation of the circulation dynamics of a Louisiana bar-built estuary. M. S. thesis, Louisiana State University, Baton Rouge, Louisiana.

Boris, J. P., and D. L. Book. 1973. Flux-corrected transport, I, SHAST: A fluid transport algorithm that works. J. Computational Physics. 11, 39-69.

Byrne, P., M. Borengasser, G. Drew, R. A. Muller, B. L. Smith, Jr., and C. Wax. 1976. Barataria Basin : Hydrologic and climatologic processes. Louisiana State University, Center for Wetland Resources. Sea Grant Pub. No. LSU-T-76-010.

Elliott, A. J. and R. O. Reid. 1976. Salinity induced horizontal estuarine circulation. J. Waterways, Harbors and Coastal Engineering Division. WW4, 425-442.

Farrow, D. E. and D. P. Stevens. 1995. A new tracer advection scheme for Bryan and Cox type ocean general circulation models. J. Physical Oceanography. 25, 1731-1741.

Fisher, H. B., E. J. List, R. C. Y. Koh, J. Imberger, and N. H. Brooks. 1979. Mixing in inland and coastal waters. Academic Press, New York, 483 pp.

Geaghan, J. P. 1995. Caernarvon Project: Isohaline station salinity analysis. Unpublished Report. Department of experimental Statistics, Louisiana State Univeristy, 26 pp.

Gerdes, R., C. Koberle, and J. Willebrand. 1991. The influence of numerical advection schemes on the results of ocean general circulation models. Climate Dynamics. 5, 211-226.

Grant, W. D. and O. S. Madsen. 1979. Combined wave and current interaction with a rough bottom. J. Geophy. Res. 84, 1979-1808.

Grammeltvedt, A. 1969. A survey of finite-difference schemes for the primitive equations for a barotropic fluid. Mon. Wea. Rev. 97, 384-404.

Hart, W. E. 1978. A numerical study of currents, water surface elevations, and energy dissipation in Chandeleur-Breton Sound, Louisiana. Ph. D. dissertation, Louisisna State University, Baton Rouge, Louisiana, 97 pp.

52

Hasumi, H. and N. Suginohara. 1999. Sensitivity of a global circulation model to tracer advection schemes. J. Phys. Oceanogr. 29, 2730-2740.

Hsu, Y. and A. Arakawa. 1990. Numerical modeling of the atmosphere with an isentropic vertical coordinate. Mon. Wea. Rev. 118, 1933-1959.

Inoue, M., W. J. Wiseman, Jr. and D. Park. 1998. Coastal marine Environmental Modeling. OCS Study MMS 98-0052. U. S. Dept. of the Interiors, Minerals management Service, Gulf of Mexico OCS Region, New Orleans, La. 133 pp.

Inoue, M. and W. J. Wiseman, Jr. 2000. Transport, stirring and mixing processes in a Louisiana estuary: A model study. Estuarine. Coastal and Shelf Science. 50, 449-466.

Kapolnai, A., F. E. Werner and J. O. Blanton. 1996. Circulation, mixing, and exchange processing in the vicinity of tidal inlets: A numerical study. J. Geophys. Res. **101**, 14253-14268.

Leendertse, J. J. 1967. Aspects of a computational model for long period water wave propagation. RM-5294-PR, Rand Corporation, Santa Monica, CA., 165 pp.

Leonard, B. P. 1979. A stable and accurate convective modeling procedure based on quadratic upstream interpolation. Comput. Methods Appl. Mech. Eng. 19, 59-98.

Leonard, B. P., M. K. MacVean and A. P. Lock. 1993. Positivity-preserving numerical schemes for multidimensional advection. NASA Tech. Memo. 106055, ICOMP-93-05, 62 pp.

Luettich, R. A., Jr., D. R. F. Harleman, and L. Somlyody. 1990. Dynamic behavior of suspended sediment concentration in a shallow lake perturbed by episodic wind effects. Limnol. Oceanogr. 35, 1050-1067.

Maier-Reimer, E., U. Mikolajewicz, and K. Hasselmann. 1993. Mean circulation of the Hamburg LSG OGCM and its sensitivity to the themohaline surface forcing. J. Phys. Oceanogr. 23, 731-757.

Mesinger, F. and A. Arakawa. 1976. Numerical methods used in atmospheric models. GARP Pub. Ser. 17, World Meteorological Organization, Geneva, Switzerland, 64 pp.

Okubo, A. 1971. Oceanic diffusion diagrams. Deep-Sea Research. 18, 789-802.

Okubo, A. 1973. Effect of shoreline irregularities on streamwise dispersion in estuaries and other embayments. Netherlands Journal of Sea Research. 6, 213-224.

Okubo, A. 1974. Some speculations on oceanic diffusion diagrams. Rapp. P.-v. Reun. Cons. Int. Explor. Mer. 167, 77-85.

Park, D. 1998. A modeling study of the Barataria Basin system. M. S. thesis, Louisiana State University. Baton Rouge, LA. 133 pp.

Ridderinkhof, H. 1990. Residual currents and mixing in the Wadden Sea. Ph. D. dissertation, Utrecht Univ., Utrecht, Netherlands. 91 pp.

Sanderson, B. G., A. Okubo, I. T. Webster, S. Kioroglou, S. and R. Appeldoorn. 1995. Observations and idealized models of dispersion on the southwestern Puerto Rican insular shelf. Mathematical Computer Modelling. 21(6), 39-63.

Signell, R. P., R. C. Beardsley, H. C. Graber and A. Capotondi. 1990. Effect of wave-current interaction on wind-driven circulation in narrow, shallow embayments. J. Geophys. Res. 95(6) 9671-9678.

Signell, R. P. and B. Butman. 1992. Modeling tidal exchange and dispersion in Boston Harbor. J. Geophys. Res. 97, 15591-15606.

Smith, J. D. 1977. Modelling of sediment transport on continental shelves. In (E. D. Golderg, I. N. McCave and J. J. O'Brien, eds.) The Sea, Vol. 6. John Wiley and Sons, New York. 539-577.

Smolarkiewcz, P. K. 1984. A fully multidimensional positive definite advection transport algorithm with small implicit diffusion. J. Computational Physics. 54, 325-362.

Takacs, L. L. 1985. A two-step scheme for the advection equation with minimized dissipation and dispersion errors. Mon. Wea. Rev. 113, 1050-1065.

UNESCO. 1981. Tenth report of the joint panel on oceanographic tables and standards. UNESCO Tech. Rep. In Marine Science No. 36. UNESCO, Paris, 25 pp.

Wiseman, W. J. Jr. and M. Inoue. 1994. Salinity variability and transport processes. pp. 3.1-3.31. In H. H. Roberts. Critical physical processes of wetland loss. Final Report to U. S. Geological Survey. Coastal Studies Institute, Louisiana State University, Baton Rouge, LA.

Wiseman, Jr. Wm. J. and E. M. Swenson. 1989. Modelling the effects of produced water discharges on estuarine salinity, In Environmental impact of produced water discharges in coastal Louisiana. In D. F. Boesch and N. N. Rabalais. Report to the Louisiana Division of the Mid-Continental Oil and Gas Association. Louisiana Universities Marine Consortium. Chauvin, LA. 287 pp.

54

Wolanski, E. and P. B. Ridd. 1986. Tidal mixing and trapping in mangrove swamps. Estuarine, Coastal and Shelf Science. **23**, 759-771.

The Department of the Interior Mission

As the Nation's principal conservation agency, the Department of the Interior has responsibility for most of our nationally owned public lands and natural resources. This includes fostering sound use of our land and water resources; protecting our fish, wildlife, and biological diversity; preserving the environmental and cultural values of our national parks and historical places; and providing for the enjoyment of life through outdoor recreation. The Department assesses our energy and mineral resources and works to ensure that their development is in the best interests of all our people by encouraging stewardship and citizen participation in their care. The Department also has a major responsibility for American Indian reservation communities and for people who live in island territories under U.S. administration.

The Minerals Management Service Mission

As a bureau of the Department of the Interior, the Minerals Management Service's (MMS) primary responsibilities are to manage the mineral resources located on the Nation's Outer Continental Shelf (OCS), collect revenue from the Federal OCS and onshore Federal and Indian lands, and distribute those revenues.

Moreover, in working to meet its responsibilities, the **Offshore Minerals Management Program** administers the OCS competitive leasing program and oversees the safe and environmentally sound exploration and production of our Nation's offshore natural gas, oil and other mineral resources. The MMS **Minerals Revenue Management** meets its responsibilities by ensuring the efficient, timely and accurate collection and disbursement of revenue from mineral leasing and production due to Indian tribes and allottees, States and the U.S. Treasury.

The MMS strives to fulfill its responsibilities through the general guiding principles of: (1) being responsive to the public's concerns and interests by maintaining a dialogue with all potentially affected parties and (2) carrying out its programs with an emphasis on working to enhance the quality of life for all Americans by lending MMS assistance and expertise to economic development and environmental protection.